The Inner Cat

Also by Carole C. Wilbourn
CATS PREFER IT THIS WAY

STEIN AND DAY
Publishers/New York

The Inner Cat

A
New Approach
to Cat Behavior

Carole C. Wilbourn

First published in 1978
Copyright © 1978 by Carole C. Wilbourn
All rights reserved
Drawings and design by Barbara Huntley
Printed in the United States of America
Stein and Day/*Publishers*/Scarborough
House,
Briarcliff Manor, N.Y. 10510

*Library of Congress Cataloging in Publication
Data*

Wilbourn, Carole, 1940–
The inner cat.

1. Cats—Behavior.   2. Cats.
SF446.5.W54   636.8   77-20189
ISBN 0-8128-2450-4

FOR PAUL,
whose love and knowledge
have helped to nurture
The Inner Cat

Contents

Introduction

Oliver was my first cat. Other cats were part of my early childhood, but it was Oliver who shared my first apartment in Greenwich Village when I went to school at New York University. I adopted him through an ad in the *Village Voice*.

Someone else was going to adopt Oliver, but the maid threatened to move out if a cat moved in. Oliver's mother was a Siamese who had sneaked out and mated with a tomcat. The rest of the litter resembled her. Oliver looked like an ordinary tiger-and-white cat and was not snatched up like the rest of his litter mates.

He was about six weeks old when I adopted him in 1962. I knew very little about cats then. The only thing I knew was that I wanted one to live with me. Because I had a front apartment with a window facing the street, Oliver

was able to go in and out the window at will. He had a collar and name tag and I was too unaware at the time to even think that he might get hit by a taxi or harmed in some other way. Only once did he disappear for a couple of days. He returned home in the arms of a lady who told me he'd accidentally been locked in her basement.

Because I was always on a stringent budget, my eating habits were grotesque, and Oliver's diet was not much better. Dry food made up the bulk of his diet. Fortunately, Oliver's string of admirers sometimes left doggie bags in the window from Peter's Backyard restaurant. Oliver adored the treats.

It never occurred to me to adopt a friend for Oliver. After all, he was outside most of the time and he used to hang out with a big orange cat that lived across the street in the poodle shop.

When he was about two years old, he suffered a urinary attack, which a neighborhood veterinarian treated. Oliver was hospitalized for a few days, but I was able to visit him.

In 1965 I married someone who had a two-year-old Siamese named Sambo. I had given Sambo to him as a birthday present when Sambo was still a kitten. My marriage was a drastic change for Oliver. Not only did he lose his open window on Tenth Street but he had to share an apartment with Sambo, who was both antagonistic and aggressive toward him. I did my best to try to encourage their friendship but, looking back, I did all the wrong things. Theirs was not a friendship. They simply shared the same apartment. Sambo was indeed the dominant one. He was sleek and wiry, whereas Oliver was big and never too graceful. Sambo demanded affection whereas Oliver often withdrew, and I wasn't always sensitive enough to draw him out.

In the next few years Oliver was treated for a few

urinary attacks. He still ate some dry food, and I was told to eliminate this from his diet and to keep him on medication for a while.

It was during this time that my interest in cats spiraled. Very often I would find an orphan cat, stash him away in my walk-in closet, and put an ad in the *Village Voice* for him. The orphan would be separated from Oliver and Sambo, but they were quite aware there was another cat around. Their disposition always improved after the other cat was adopted. Aside from placing cats, I did volunteer work for various animal organizations that sponsored neutering and humane legislation.

In 1969 my marriage ended and my life became hectic for a while. Again, Oliver was hospitalized for a urinary attack. Although Oliver and Sambo were still together, their relationship wasn't any closer.

Paul came into my life in 1970. I was an avid cat enthusiast by then. It was a sick black cat that brought us together. Paul was working for my veterinarian, and I was urged by a friend to make an appointment with him. My friend was positive I'd appreciate his looks and his way with animals. She was 100 percent correct. That first visit was to be the start of a relationship that continues and takes on a deeper dimension each day.

In the beginning Paul liked cats but was not particularly a cat enthusiast. As our relationship grew, he became very close to Oliver and Sambo. They responded well to Paul but it still didn't help their relationship. By the fall of 1970 Oliver became fatally sick and passed on of leukemia. It took me a while before I could realistically deal with his loss. The pain was too piercing.

After some time had passed, I realized there were so many things I could have done to make Oliver's life happier and fuller. When it became apparent that Sambo needed a companion, I knew there had to be a better way to introduce two cats than the way I brought Oliver and Sambo together. Furthermore, I knew I had to figure out the best way, so that I could give the future relationship all the support it needed. Fortunately, I was able to construct a good method of introduction (described in Chapter 3), and the new kitten Mugsy was all that Sambo needed. The more I saw Sambo and his kitten interacting together, the more I thought about how great a factor stress was in Oliver's life.* His kittenhood got off to an insecure start because he was unlike the rest of his litter. He was rejected by the people who almost adopted him because of their maid. The diet I fed him caused him physical stress, and hospitalization added mental stress. He had never had his own companion before Sambo, which made his acceptance of Sambo harder. These were only the beginnings of the factors that contributed to Oliver's emotional stress.

The years passed and Sambo's first kitten Mugsy vanished when we were in Malibu. Sambo's reaction was dramatic. He cried constantly and didn't want to let us out of his sight. He was so lonely for Mugsy. Finally, Sambo was given a new kitten whom we called Mugsy-Baggins. Now Sambo had his own friend again. Around this time Paul and I began traveling a lot and it became apparent that the cats were much happier if they traveled with us. I had never given Oliver the opportunity to do this. I realized that being left alone had more than likely contributed to Oliver's lack of confidence.

By the time Paul and I opened The Cat Practice in 1973, I'd encountered many, many cats. With so many of them, as with Oliver, their person's lack of knowledge of the

* *Stress:* any stimulus, as fear or pain, that disturbs or interferes with normal physiological equilibrium of an organism; physical, mental or emotional strain or tension.—*The Random House Dictionary of the English Language*, Random House, 1967.

cat's needs had precipitated similar kinds of physical and emotional problems. It became very clear to me that urinary problems are triggered primarily by stress. Perhaps the most difficult thing for me to accept was that, like Oliver, so many cats that develop leukemia and other types of cancer have experienced excessive emotional stress. I couldn't help thinking how traumatic it must have been for Oliver to move to an apartment that he had to share with a strange cat, and where he could no longer enjoy the freedom of going outdoors.

In the past four-and-a-half years we've treated over seven thousand patients. Among these patients there have been many different kinds of behavioral disorders. The cases I've been able to treat successfully have made me very happy. But for those that I haven't, I can only hope that time will bring the answers. The field of feline behavior has only begun to be explored. Oliver was the catalyst for me.

By setting up The Cat Practice as more than a veterinary clinic, we feel we are providing total cat care. Paul provides the medical expertise, and I deal with the behavioral and emotional aspects; in this way we get in touch with the inner cat. I hope you, the reader, will be able to benefit from our experiences and, in turn, will find answers to many of the day-to-day questions you have about living with your cats.

The Inner Cat

Chapter 1

Everyday Living

It's only the middle of December and the weather has been abominable. You find you've been spending most of your evenings indoors and you're getting somewhat bored. Your neighbor is always asking you over to see what wonderful things her cat is doing. The last time you lived with a cat was when you were a toddler and your cat memories are vague.

You decide maybe it would be fun to add a cat to your life. Then you'd have companionship whenever you wanted it. After all, a cat pretty well takes care of itself, you think.

Yes, a cat would certainly add flair to your everyday living, but there are some major things you must consider before taking responsibility for another life besides your own. First, you must realize that adopting a cat is a total commitment. The cat will be dependent on you physically and emotionally. If you're a compulsively neat person who must have everything in place and the thought of cleaning a litter box repels you, don't adopt a cat. If you're expecting a cat to be like the dog you've always wanted but could never have, forget it. Cats and dogs are both domesticated animals, but their similarity ends there. If you tend to be impressionable and change your mind radically from moment to moment, don't adopt a cat on an impulse. A cat is not a disposable object, but a living being with feelings.

If now you're still sure you want to adopt a cat, you have to decide the age, sex, and type of cat you want. Chances are, if you like kids and don't mind a high energy level, a kitten would be fun. Try to adopt one that is at least two months old. The older the kitten is, the better its chances are of being healthy and well-adjusted. It would actually be best to adopt two kittens so that they can play and interact together. If you'd prefer to live with a female, adopt a female; if not, a male. It's impossible to make rigid generalizations about either sex. As for type of cat, if a long-haired cat appeals to you, you must be prepared to brush and comb it each day. If not, its fur will become tangled and the kitten will become uncomfortable and unhappy. Long-haired cats also require an occasional bath. If you're not into fastidious grooming, a short-haired kitten would be best. You would still have to brush it frequently, but short hair is much easier to care for. Also, shedding from a long-haired cat is greater.

It's a beautiful and delightful experience to watch a kitten grow up, but your economic and day-to-day responsibility is greater than with an older cat:

1. A kitten must be vaccinated against distemper at six weeks, eight weeks, twelve weeks, and sixteen weeks of age. Only then can you be certain that it has received adequate immunity. Every year following, only an annual booster vaccination is necessary.

2. A kitten must be vaccinated against respiratory vi-

ruses at two months of age and again at three months. After this, a booster vaccination is needed once a year.

3. A kitten must be fed four times a day until it's four months old, three times a day until it's six months old, and twice a day from then on. Small frequent feedings are necessary because a kitten's stomach is small.

4. A kitten needs more attention than an adolescent or older cat. You can't expect to leave it alone for long periods of time without coming home to a kitten that's falling all over you for attention. Also, it wouldn't be too surprising if the kitten had done a bit of housewrecking just to stay amused. You might even be awakened during the night by the kitten kneading in your hair or sucking on your ear.

If you are not devastated by these considerations, perhaps a kitten is best for you. But again, let me recommend that you adopt two kittens so your kitten will not be deprived of companionship.

If you prefer mature company and you have no special desire to take part in kittenhood, an adolescent of several months or an older cat would be best for you. Again, whether it's long- or short-haired depends upon the amount of grooming you want to do and the amount of shedding you can realistically cope with.

Which sex to adopt is purely a matter of personal preference. If you adopt a male before he's sexually mature, it will be necessary to have him altered when he comes of age (generally, anytime between seven months and a year; sometimes it's as early as five to six months). His sexual maturity will be indicated by consistently strong-smelling urine, frequent crying, and rough playing. If you adopt a female before she's sexually mature, she should be spayed after her first heat (which could be as early as five-and-a-half months or as late as a year).

Occasionally, a female may have a silent heat but, ordinarily, there's no way to mistake a cat in heat. She may start off by simply losing her appetite, followed by pitiful crying. Then you'll notice that she's sensitive when you pet her on the lower part of her back. As you touch her she appears to shiver. Soon she's crouching or rolling from side to side. Her motion may even look like a sensual shimmy.

If you know that you just won't be able to deal with your cat's surgery, a neutered male or female would be ideal for you. Whichever gender you decide upon, your cat should be vaccinated against distemper and respiratory viruses. Then he'll need a booster every year following to boost his immunity, whether he remains a house cat or goes outdoors. Once more I must repeat that it's best to adopt two cats so there will be constant companionship. (For clarity's sake, I'll use the masculine pronoun form. I'll also use "cat" instead of "kitten.")

Once you've decided what type of cat you want to live with, it's most important to know where you can adopt one. You might try your local shelter or humane society. Generally, these cats are caged and the sooner they get adopted, the better for them. Check the pet adoption column in your local newspapers and the bulletin board at your neighborhood supermarket. If you want a special breed of cat, you might even put an ad in the paper or at your neighborhood grocery.

Don't run off to the nearest pet shop and buy a cat. With all the homeless and abandoned cats and kittens, there's just no excuse for profit making. Don't support people who are interested primarily in the economics rather than the welfare of the animals.

When you are adopting your cat, make sure your choice is alert, has bright eyes, and glossy fur. You want to try to make sure you are starting off with a healthy cat, though this is something about which you can never be positive, because sometimes a disaster can be incubating and won't show up until later.

Before you bring your cat home, it would be best to have him examined by a veterinarian and given whatever vaccinations are essential at that time. Also, this way the veterinarian will be able to follow your cat's progress from the beginning. Your vet will probably recommend that a stool sample be taken, to check for parasites.

There are certain preparations you will have to make prior to the big homecoming:

1. Purchase a plastic litter pan, or dishpan, and kitty litter from your supermarket. The ground-clay or sand type of litter works best. You will also need a plastic scooper to scoop out the dirty litter. Generally, it's most convenient to keep the litter box by the toilet so you can flush away the dirty litter. It is best to scoop out the used litter frequently and to empty and clean the entire box once a week.

2. Food bowls should not be made of plastic because sometimes the hydrocarbons in the plastic will react with the skin, causing a chin rash. There should be a bowl for food and one for water.

3. A commercial cat food that contains beef or beef by-products is best. Organ meats or poultry can be supplemented, but some cats will not eat canned chicken or turkey. Fish is acceptable as an occasional meal. Tuna should be avoided because of its allergenic characteristics. Cats are carnivores and, though vegetables are optional, don't try to make your cat a vegetarian. If you'd prefer to cook meat or poultry for your cat, that's fine. However, cat food that includes meat or meat by-products (not specifically beef) is not recommended because any low-grade meat can be included. Horse meat and pork are commonly used ingredients and

some cats are allergic to them. Dry and semi-moist foods are good supplements but should not provide the major part of your cat's diet. Cooked chicken necks and backs are perfect for good gum exercise. Cheese and yogurt are excellent snacks. Olives (pitless) and cantaloupe are often good aphrodisiacs.

4. It is only natural for a cat to exercise its claws by scratching. That's why you must provide a sturdy and adequate scratching post. The best commercial post is made by the Felix company in Seattle, Washington. They make a sisal-covered post filled with catnip which presently sells for $14.00. You can write to them at 416 Smith Street, Seattle, Washington, 98109. If you decide to build a post, make sure you use scratchy material and line the inside with catnip; the base must be sturdy so that the post won't fall over when it is used.

5. You might purchase a few catnip toys and some catnip. The best catnip can be purchased from an herb store or ordered from Felix. It's even possible to grow your own catnip. Catnip is a naturally occurring herb whose active ingredient is not harmful. For most cats it's a pleasant aphrodisiac and a healthy way to work off energy. However, some cats don't respond to catnip at all. Catnip stays fresher if kept in the refrigerator.

6. If you decide to buy a basket for your cat to sleep in, don't be surprised if the cat prefers your bed. However, if you place the basket in the sun, it might turn out to be a daytime resting place.

7. You'll need to purchase a commercial carrier from the pet department of your local department store or pet-supply store. The model with the wire top is best. Be sure to line the carrier with strips of newspaper in case there's an accident. Otherwise the carrier may become badly soiled.

8. Be certain that all your windows are closed. If you must keep your windows open, use half screens, but make sure they fit securely in place. Although a cat's balance is remarkable, its depth perception is not. All it takes is one wrong step and down the cat goes—sometimes never to return. Cats don't always land on their feet.

9. Move your plants and fragile ornaments to safety. It may be necessary to hang your plants if they become in demand.

10. Buy a rubber brush for a short-haired cat. You'll need three sizes of combs if your cat is long-haired.

11. If your cat is going to be going outdoors, provide him with a collar and name tag (see Chapter 6).

Now you have your place in order, you've adopted your cat, and you've arrived home. Breathe freely, smile, and talk softly to your new friend. The following instructions will help make the homecoming easier and happier.

1. Set the carrier on the bathroom floor next to the litter box and close the door.

2. Open the carrier so your cat can come out at his own speed. Meanwhile you can be talking slowly and gently. A trip to the litter box may be in order. Don't forget to scoop and flush away the dirty litter.

3. After your cat has become familiar with the litter box, you can open the bathroom door and allow him to explore the rest of your home. Be sure he discovers his scratching post and feeding bowls.

4. Water can be available, but don't offer any food for at

least a few hours. By then the immediate excitement should be over.

5. Don't be surprised if your cat refuses food or chooses to hide the first day. However, if this behavior continues, consult your veterinarian.

By the end of the day you should be very pleased with your new lifestyle. True, you have an added responsibility, but you have also made a start to a fuller and happier life.

By the end of a month you're already a veteran cat person, but there are still things you should understand so that you can keep everyday stress to a minimum.

If you are awakened each morning by a friendly paw dragged across your mouth, or four iron paws across your head, or a dead weight resting on your bladder, try to stay relaxed. Calmly stroke your cat, tell him how tired you are, and explain that if you can sleep a little longer, his breakfast will taste much better. No doubt he'll stay hungry, but he may take pity and permit you to sleep a little longer. True, he won't understand what you're saying but he'll respond to your low-key energy.

When you finally do stagger out of bed, start by petting your cat and making him feel good. Even if you're feeling down, positive energy can improve your spirits While you're stumbling around in the bathroom, make sure the litter box is clean. Often, the box can take on a truly unappealing dimension during the night. No doubt he'll christen the box immediately. But why not; that is why you cleaned it. Make sure you clean out the food bowls before adding new food, and don't forget to provide fresh water. If you must leave the house shortly after, never forget to say goodbye to your cat and assure him you'll be home later. Face-to-face farewells eliminate the possibility of your cat's being locked away in a closet or drawer while you're away all day.

Protect your cat from creating mischief out of boredom while you're away. Don't allow carelessness to cause you unhappy moments.

1. If your cat's a plant lover, hang your plants so they'll be out of temptation's reach. Some cats find nature irresistible. Don't tempt him by creating a situation in which you'll be fuming and he'll be confused.

2. If your cat tends to be wary of strangers and a repairman or someone else is expected while you're away, close your cat in another room with his favorite toys and necessities within reach. If this is impossible, try to have a friend be present or give your cat a tranquilizer (one prescribed by your veterinarian).

3. If you'll be home after dark, leave a light on. Although cats are nocturnal, it's difficult for them to see in complete darkness. Some cats enjoy sitting under a light because of its warmth.

4. Don't leave pins or needles within reach for your cat to accidentally swallow. He could suffer serious medical complications.

5. Never leave windows open from the bottom (I can't stress this enough). Cats don't have good depth perception. One false leap for a passing bird or object and down he goes. Your cat might not survive such a fall.

6. Keep your garbage out of reach. Why give your cat an opportunity to have a go at it?

Don't be surprised if caring for your cat improves your housekeeping techniques. If you leave clothing around, your cat will probably sprawl out on it. If you do your part, you can be sure he'll do his.

Greet your cat immediately when you return home at

night. Let him know how much you've missed him, and you can even air your complaints. Your cat won't mind as long as you hurry to check his litter box so that it will be clean for his next visit. Most of all—if it's feeding time, don't delay. After your cat has finished eating, be sure to stroke and comfort him. Don't forget to tell him how beautiful he is. Maybe he won't understand the word "beautiful," but he'll respond to the feeling you give off when you say it.

Now you can safely begin to make your own dinner without your cat's getting in the way. However, if he insists upon jumping up to sample the ingredients, try giving him some catnip or his favorite toy as a diversion. You might even offer him a sample of what you're cooking. If you're lucky, he won't like it. If he just won't give up and has already eaten all his own food, give him more. He may still be hungry. Lock him in another room only if you've exhausted every other solution. Don't set up a frustrating situation.

When bedtime arrives and your cat runs back and forth across your body with no sign of stopping, try the following techniques:

1. Let your body relax and breathe deeply. This might influence him to do the same.

2. Offer him a snack or some catnip. He may just be trying to get your attention because he's hungry.

3. Chase him around playfully until he loses his flash of energy.

If all these alternatives fail, put him on the bed and stroke him until he relaxes. You might even have to squeeze him firmly but gently, which will allow the pent-up energy to be released. By this time you should both be thoroughly exhausted and ready for a pleasant night's sleep.

Punky is a two-year-old Siamese cat whose bedtime performance was devastating to her people. Every night at bedtime she would dash around the apartment howling and sometimes even hurling herself at the bedroom blinds. The other cat in the household would sometimes become startled by Punky's behavior but fortunately would not follow her example. I was able to recommend to her people the following treatment, which cured Punky's problem:

1. A bedtime snack.

2. Chasing Punky around the apartment earlier in the evening.

3. Playing chase and fetch-it with her.

4. Allowing her to take strolls in the hall of the apartment building.

5. Holding her tightly when she cried.

Because Punky is a young and very hyper and wired cat, it's very necessary for her to release a lot of energy throughout the day. When her people made a concerted effort to help Punky release her energy before bedtime, her nightly extravaganza was soon shortened to a few bedtime leaps and bounds.

Some cats are frightened by rain storms. If your cat is affected, pull down the blinds, turn on some quiet music, and offer him one of his favorite treats. Stroke his body gently if he's receptive, and talk slowly and soothingly. Try repeating this whenever there's a storm, and if your cat responds favorably, you'll have substituted a positive response for an unhappy one.

Firecrackers can be another source of anxiety. If they are, follow the same procedure as above. However, if your cat does not respond, consult your veterinarian about prescribing a tranquilizer. But be sure to find out what kind of reaction your cat might have to the tranquilizer. At first, most tranquilizers may affect coordination, increase appetite, and produce disorientation. So if at first your cat loses his graceful presence, talks nonstop, and eats furiously, relax and don't panic. Soon your cat will adjust to the tranquilizer's reaction and will stop fighting the unusual feeling.

Now several months have passed and you wonder how you ever lived without your cat. In fact, sometimes you think you'd like to adopt another, but you feel deep down that you can realistically provide only one cat with enough love and attention.

Then one day you are on your way to the cheese shop when an anemic-looking cat throws himself in front of you. You reach down to pet him and continue on your way but he proceeds to follow you, screaming all the way. Finally, you cross the street and when you reach the other side he's nowhere in sight. With a sigh of relief you enter the cheese shop. It's an hour later, and you're on your way home with your head filled with thoughts of how good your stomach's going to feel, when that same cat approaches you again. "Why me?" you think to yourself and you reach inside your package and break off a piece of cheese. The cat devours it and cries for more. You quickly break off a larger chunk and hurry on your way. But this time the cat follows you across the street. There's no way he's going to let you go. But what can you do to help him, you ask yourself. You know your cat would never accept him and you really don't want another cat.

First, you must decide whether, if you make the commitment to be responsible for the cat, you will be able to see it all the way through. By this I mean, will you be able to provide for him until you can find him a suitable home? This does not mean dropping him off at the nearest shelter, which is most probably overcrowded and couldn't provide the same care an individual could. There's also a great probability that the cat will become sick from cross-infection of other cats or sheer stress.

If you know you won't be able to cope with this situation, leave the cat in the street and maybe the next person will be able to offer what you could not.

If you feel you can accept the responsibility, then you wonder how you can get him home. There is a preferred way to handle such a situation. If the cat is willing, you can pick him up and carry him. It's best to wrap him in something so he feels secure and protected. It will also protect you from being accidentally scratched if he should panic.

Once you reach home, immediately isolate the cat from yours. Put him in the bathroom if that's the only available room and wash your hands before touching your cat. Be sure to move your cat's litter box and belongings to another area. The following instructions should make things easier:

1. Distract your cat with food or catnip.

2. Be sure to provide the visiting cat with a litter box. Feed him if he should start crying.

3. Don't forget to wash your hands each time you handle the cat to eliminate the possibility of spreading any infection or exciting your cat with the visitor's scent.

4. Make up signs giving the cat's description and your phone number. Post them within the area where he was found. There is the possibility that he's lost.

5. If there's no response to your signs within a few days, it is time to start thinking about potential adopters.

6. At this time, too, it would be best to have the cat checked by your veterinarian. Your vet will probably want to vaccinate him against distemper. If it turns out you've mistaken the cat's gender and this is an unspayed female, now would be the time to have her spayed. It's easier to find a home for a neutered cat.

7. It's most important that you give your cat extra attention and love so that he doesn't feel deprived or neglected. Because this is a stressful situation, you want to be positive your cat is at the top of your priority list.

8. If you've sounded out your friends and neighbors without any offers, put ads in the pet-adoption columns of your local newspaper. Be sure your copy is snappy and appealing. You might even post signs in your local supermarkets.

9. Be sure to screen any potential adopter. Find out if he or she has had cats before, if so, what happened to them, and what the person's living situation is. If you get a feeling there is instability, you'll know this won't be the right home.

10. Make sure you deliver your adoptee to his new home so you can rest assured his new environment will be right for him.

Soon your visiting cat will be adopted and you and your cat will quickly forget there was ever an intruder—that is, until you receive a card or phone call from the adoptee's new person telling you how happy they both are and that you're the one to thank.

Ever since your cat arrived, you and your neighbor have become even closer. Now you're forever filling her ears with tales of your exceptionally terrific cat. One evening you return from her apartment and you find your apartment door slightly ajar. Somehow you didn't completely close it when you went to visit. How stupid you think to yourself. You immediately push the door open and call to your cat. No answer! He must be hiding. You search the apartment, rattle the can opener, and he's still nowhere to be seen. Soon you're running down the hall and up and down the stairs frantically calling his name. He's got to be somewhere in the building. He couldn't have gotten outside to the street! Two hours later he's back in your apartment. He'd wandered into a man's apartment on the sixth floor. The man found him sleeping at the foot of his bed.

Fortunately, your cat returned home safe and sound. For awhile you were quite shaken up but there was no lasting damage. However, in the future you'll be more careful about closing your apartment door.

Since your cat has already made one disappearing act, it would be best to provide him with a collar and identification tag. There is a special safety collar available that will slip off the neck if it becomes caught on anything.

Luckily your cat did not make it out to the street and your sleuthing was minimized. The following procedure will be helpful if your cat ever actually disappears:

1. Post signs with his description and your phone number up and down the streets, inside buildings, and at stores and markets.

2. Check to see if anyone has posted signs telling that they've found your cat.

3. Contact your local shelters without delay.

4. Be sure to check the lost-and-found columns of your local newspapers. You might want to run an ad yourself. A reward is advisable.

5. Check to see if your community has a pet finder's organization. You supply them with your cat's description and, for a small fee, they thoroughly check the papers and local shelters for you. Then each day you contact them for information.

During this time it's important that you use as much constructive energy as you can in trying to find your cat. Nothing is foolish that might possibly help to bring your cat home again. When you do locate your cat, it would be best to have him checked over by your vet to be sure he's in good shape.

Siah was a California cat who spent most of his days outdoors but would return home each evening. One evening he didn't return, much to his people's sorrow. Several weeks later they received a phone call that Siah was all right. He'd been hiding under someone's house and finally hobbled out. Because his collar supplied identification, his rescuers were able to make contact. Apparently, he was hit by a car and his leg was fractured. He stayed hidden long enough for it to heal. It would never be straight, but Siah was safe.

Angel Face was an apartment cat who one day disappeared. One month later her people found her flat out in the courtyard. Evidently, she'd fallen from a window. Her jaw was broken and her lungs were partially collapsed. After a few days of hospitalization she returned home. Her people later learned that she had moved in with a family on the tenth floor and made her sky dive from their window. If Angel Face had identification or her people had posted signs, her reunion would have been quicker and less traumatic.

If you don't succeed in finding your cat, try to think that he had to move on and found someone else that he had to take care of.

One of the most important things your cat has taught you is that he doesn't belong to you. He lives with you and shares himself, but you don't or can't possess him. You are his person but not his owner. Your relationship is what you put into it. Sometimes you may feel that you do everything for him but you question what he gives in return. This is a feeling that never lasts long. All he has to do is snuggle next to you, start to purr, and your whole being melts and relaxes. Each day he teaches you how to feel deep down to your toes. It's easy for him to do this for, because he's a cat, he's full of sensitivity and feeling.

Everyday living with your cat may sometimes be puzzling or trying, but never, never unfulfilling.

Chapter 2

The Single Cat Syndrome

Everything's been going along fine for you and your cat. He sleeps with you, you chase him, he chases you. You even share your evening cookies with him. Then all of a sudden your work schedule changes. You receive word that you'll have to work overtime for at least the next month with only a few days off. With all your other activities, you realize this leaves little more than waking and sleeping time with your cat. He's always been very demanding of you and you know he's going to be affected. He'll show his anger by sulking or not running to greet you at the door. He may give you the royal brush-off and even refuse to sleep with you for several nights. On the other hand, he may go on a hunger strike for a few days. Whatever his reaction is, you know he won't be happy.

If only there were someone else who could spend time with him, you think to yourself. But right off, there's no one you can think of. All your cat-loving friends have cats of their own. The rest of your friends have kids or can just about take care of themselves. What to do?

Now's the time to be daring and aggressive. The moment has come for your cat to have his own friend. You've thought about adopting another cat before, but always fleetingly. After all, it's bad enough changing a litter box after one cat. Two cats and your place would probably smell like a barn, you tell yourself. Besides, there'd be two to feed and double the amount of care and expense, not to mention more cat fur all over your bed.

True, the litter box would get dirtier with two cats, but a scoop with the scooper and it's clean. Cat food and litter can be bought cheaper if you buy in large quantities. There are even supply places that deliver to your door. As for double the amount of fur, you'll just have to use your lint brush more often and perhaps change your sheets more frequently. Anyway, clean bedclothes are always a treat. There's no denying that veterinarian and other professional services may be doubled but, hopefully, your cats will stay healthy.

The amount of love and pleasure you'll receive from adopting a second cat far outweighs your objections. No longer can you delude yourself into thinking you can be all and everything to your cat. Human companionship is important but does not fully satisfy your cat's need to romp and communicate with his own species. He needs a buddy to stimulate his imagination, make his food more inviting, and provide him with endless hours of fun and games.

Perhaps you've noticed your cat sometimes appears to be restless and very set in his ways. Having his own friend will help him to become more adaptable to new situations instead of being inflexible. An indoors cat can easily become bored and frustrated. He may resort to destructive tactics for extra attention even if it's negative attention.

Toby is a one-year-old cat who lives with his person,

Hank. Hank found Toby several months ago as a tomcat and soon after had him altered. Despite the fact that he was altered and his urine tests were normal, Toby continued to urinate all around the apartment. His favorite place was a shaggy rug. Toby got a lot of attention from Hank, but Hank was often away from home. It was obvious that Toby was manifesting his need for attention by his indiscriminate urinating. I recommended that Hank send the rug to be cleaned and laundered but, most important, that he adopt a companion for Toby. If Toby had a friend to interact with, his need for attention would be fulfilled.

Boredom and frustration can often precipitate anxiety attacks that cause a cat to become aggressive and hostile toward people.

Gordon is a one-year-old cat who would bite his people when he became excited, but most of the time his interactions with them were pleasing and compatible. They were justified, however, in not being able to trust him. Gordon started this habit at the same time he reached sexual maturity.

I explained to his people that when he became overstimulated he couldn't handle his high energy level and it would cause him to bite. If he had a kitten to interact with, he would be able to release this energy in a natural way. Soon after, his people adopted a kitten for Gordon and he is now able to release his energy in interactions with his kitten, Earle.

Minina is a black four year old who did well with her person, Jean, but was miserable to Jean's relatives and friends. She resented Jean's interacting with anyone but her. Minina had to be locked in the bedroom when anyone came to visit so that she wouldn't have the opportunity to attack. Taking her to the vet was always a trying event because Minina could be examined only under anesthesia.

It wasn't until Jean adopted Copain, a three-month-old

kitten who Minina grew to adore, that she gradually relaxed and was not threatened by intrusions of other people into the household. Copain provided her with a source of entertaining companionship. Now she had someone besides Jean she could interact with without being threatened. Copain was dependent upon her and she was in charge.

When visitors came by, she had Copain to keep her occupied. She did not have to depend upon Jean for affection. Before Copain, Jean was the only one Minina could trust. Now she could work out all her pent-up frustrations and fears by wrestling and romping with Copain. He provided her with round-the-clock companionship. She still needed Jean's love and attention but Copain was Minina's very own.

Sometimes a single cat will tend to interact erratically with his people and be very frightened of visitors.

Snoopy is a five-year-old cat who is very fearful of visitors. His interactions with his people are limited. He doesn't like to be held and prefers to play rough. At night he sleeps by his people's feet. Sometimes when he becomes excited he runs around in circles almost as if he were having a convulsion.

Because Snoopy doesn't have a friend to interact with, his energy becomes bottled up. When he becomes overstimulated, the energy explodes and causes him to run around in circles. (If this condition were allowed to continue, it could precipitate a convulsionary disorder.)

I recommended that an adopted kitten would provide Snoopy with the release he needed so that he could function on a day-to-day basis without being frustrated. His kitten would be a natural outlet for his energy. As his relationship with his kitten matured, so would his acceptance of closer contact with his people and visitors.

The absence of a companion can often cause a cat to be

self-destructive. Some cats internalize their frustration and may finally manifest it by tearing at their skin.

Sobriety is a spayed three-year-old tiger that lives with her person, Barbara. Sobriety's problem started when Barbara moved to a new apartment and also began to socialize more. It was then that Sobriety started tearing away at her skin. Sobriety's destructive behavior was partially alleviated by giving her Valium to relieve her anxiety and an anti-inflammatory medication to soothe the itching. Sobriety's cure was adopting a kitten that took her mind off herself.

Toby, Minina, and Sobriety all shared one common characteristic: the inability to relieve their anxiety constructively. When their anxiety became overwhelming, they started feeling bothered and uneasy. Each cat had a weak spot, better described as a target, that the anxiety would affect. You might compare it to a nervous person whose head starts to throb whenever anxiety or frustration begins.

Toby's target was his bladder. Although clinically it was normal, whenever he became upset his bladder ached. When his bladder became uncomfortable, he indicated his distress by urinating here, there, and everywhere. This was his way of relieving anxiety when he felt stress.

Sobriety's target was her skin. Whenever she became anxious, her skin would itch. She would scratch and tear away at it to stop the itching. Perhaps you know people who bite their nails to the quick whenever they're frustrated. There are many people, as well, who have severe skin problems because of self-destructive scratching.

Minina's target was other people. They threatened her relationship with Jean and the only way she could deal with the feeling was to victimize them. Only then was her frustration energy allayed.

With all three cats, their anxiety was triggered by the

frustration of feeling neglected. The pent-up energy mounted and there was no constructive way to release it, so it was finally transferred to their targets. This is what caused their destructive behavior. Their source of anxiety was their need for attention. Companionship filled that need, dissipated the anxiety, and provided a constructive release for their energy. Whenever they felt a need to be noticed and their person was not around, they could interact with their companion.

Your cat may never develop any of these symptoms, but why take a chance. Don't let your cat experience the "single cat syndrome" any longer. Why deny him the companionship he deserves? Both your cat and you will derive pleasure and happiness from a new cat. Don't procrastinate any longer!

25

Chapter 3

Introducing New Feline Members into the Household

So you're ready to take the big plunge! At last you've decided to adopt that long-needed companion. You're off to a good start. But you can't just bring in anybody and have confidence that your cat will accept the newcomer. There's a special way to go about it to make the companion's debut as happy and unstressful as possible.

The first important factor to be considered is your cat's personality. You must try to complement it as closely as possible. It would be senseless to adopt a companion that would only be a constant threat to him. You wouldn't want to bring in an older, aggressive male if your cat had a similar personality. You might compare the match to that of two confirmed bachelors trying to live in close harmony.

If your cat is over a year old, there will be a quicker adjustment period if you adopt a kitten, because kittens are more adaptable. Gender is not important. However, if your cat happens to be mellow and even-tempered, he will adjust to an older cat or to any type of kitten.

1. If your cat has a hostile, aggressive personality, he needs a kitten that prefers cats to people. Such a kitten is cat oriented and will instinctively turn to your cat for recognition and then later to you. Why adopt a people-oriented kitten that would be constantly jumping into your lap? You can be sure your cat would be furious, especially if you showered the kitten with attention.

2. A shy and sensitive cat also needs a cat-oriented kitten, so that his position won't be threatened. Don't provide your cat with a companion with whom he'll constantly have to compete for attention. A cat-oriented kitten will rely on your cat at first. By the time the kitten turns your way, their relationship will already be well-established.

How to Recognize a Cat-oriented Kitten

A cat-oriented kitten will be more interested in interacting with other kittens or cats than with people. When you go to pet him, he'll hiss at you or avoid your overtures. If you end up adopting an untamed kitten that was rescued from the street, you can be sure it will be cat oriented.

Whether you adopt your cat or kitten from a shelter, from someone's home, or from the street, you must take him to your vet to be examined, vaccinated, and checked for worms. Don't take the chance of exposing your healthy cat to a sick one. Ideally, it would be best to keep the newcomer at a friend's house for two weeks. If the newcomer is incubating anything infectious, it should be apparent by that time. You could then have it treated and your mind would be at ease.

Now you've carefully followed all the preceding instructions and the day of confrontation has arrived. There's a desirable way to go about the introduction.

Introduction Day

A. Inflate your cat's ego with love and praise. Tell him how much you adore him and give him lots of hugs. Don't skimp on your affection.

B. Tell your cat how he needs his own friend. No more lonely hours! Mention how good he'll feel molding a protégé in his own paw-prints.

C. Be sure to feed him his favorite treats for breakfast and save some for the encounter.

Whatever you do, don't bring the newcomer in yourself. Your cat must not feel that you are responsible for this sudden intrusion in his life. You cannot just bring the newcomer in, plop him down in front of your cat, and expect them to be off to a perfect start. There's a preferred way to go about the introduction.

Introducing the Newcomer

1. Have a neutral party bring in the newcomer. If the party is someone your cat is very fond of, he may feel slighted.

2. It's preferable for the newcomer to be in a cat carrier with a wire top so that your cat can observe him. The carrier should be lined with strips of newspaper in case the newcomer has an accident.

3. Some of the strips of newspaper (if clean) can be discreetly placed on the floor where your cat will find them. From them he'll be able to get a good whiff of the newcomer until he decides to go closer to the carrier.

4. You should be oblivious to the new arrival even if he's staring you right in the face. This would be a good time to join your guest in some light refreshment to preoccupy your mind with eating.

5. Don't discuss how your cat's going to react. Talk about anything that will get your mind off the encounter. A light, cheerful subject is best.

6. When your cat's good and ready, he'll strut over to inspect the newcomer. Don't be surprised if he's sniffing and hissing at the same time. Breathe deeply and concentrate on your juicy conversation. You don't want to pass your nervousness on to your cat.

7. Don't offer your cat any words of encouragement. If you interfere, your cat will react negatively. It must be his decision.

8. The newcomer should remain in the carrier for at least two hours. This way your cat will feel he has the upper hand.

9. After the two hours, lure your cat away from the carrier with food or catnip. While you're distracting him, your friend can unfasten the carrier so that your cat won't feel you're responsible when the newcomer pops out.

10. Don't be surprised if there are inflated tails, hissing, and even puffed-up bodies. In case of a bad skirmish, a spray of water will cool things out. You can't expect the relationship to be an instant success. If your cat should simply decide he's going to ignore the newcomer by retreating to another room the moment after the arrival, casually drop some of the newspaper from the newcomer's carrier in the room with your cat. If he still

insists on being alone, when the two hours are up have your friend open the carrier and the newcomer will take it from there. Don't try to sneak in pats with the newcomer. Your cat will only have to smell your hands to know you've deceived him.

Once the newcomer is on the loose, you must not give in to your instinctive urge to feel sorry for him because nobody loves him. Remember that the newcomer is your cat's friend and it's up to your cat to offer any attention. If you make a fuss over the newcomer, you'll be sure to offend your cat and he'll be doubly sure to stay clear of the newcomer. Your cat must make the fuss, not you. Don't lavish attention on the newcomer until your cat has fully accepted him. Don't try to force them together so that they will become friends faster. The pacing is your cat's choice, and if he chooses to take his time, nothing will hurry him.

Refer to the newcomer as your cat's friend or kitten, even if the newcomer is an older cat. Your cat won't understand what you're saying but will sense what you're feeling by the tone of your voice and the energy from your body. In turn, it will give him a good feeling and enable him to relax and not feel threatened by the newcomer.

Reinforcement

Make your cat responsible for any praise you give the newcomer, because your cat is in charge. For example: "What a smart kitten you have, but that's only because you've taught him so well." You must make it clear to your cat again and again that anything you like about the newcomer is attributable to him. Most of all, you must make sure your cat feels that he's still "number one" with you.

There's a possibility that your cat may hide for a few days or that his appetite will fall off. Don't panic! Instead, concentrate on making him feel wanted and loved. He may just be testing you and it's up to you not to let him down. When he's sure of your loyalty, he'll snap back to his usual behavior, and his adjustment to the newcomer will speed along.

Jealousy

While your two cats are developing their relationship, you may be left out of the activity for awhile. Don't feel neglected and insecure. Relax and have patience. Your cat still loves you. He hasn't forgotten you. Soon enough you'll have two cats to serenade you with their purring. One client remarked that after adopting a new kitten, she at first felt rejected. "My cat's ignoring me," she complained. "He doesn't wash my face each morning since the kitten arrived." Very shortly the situation changed. Now she had two cats climbing into bed with her and her cat went back to washing her face in the morning.

Another client was amazed to see her cat, Whiskey, allowing the newcomer to eat out of her dish. She was even more surprised the first time Whiskey washed the new kitten. "It's so marvelous the way Whiskey takes such good care of Garland. Makes it so much easier for me. Now I don't have to feel guilty if I stay out late because Whiskey has Garland to keep her company."

The added attraction of endless exercise that the newcomer offers your cat is a definite plus.

"My Katie's trimmed down now that she has her Billy to play with," a client boasted. Katie is a two-year-old cat whose litter mate died. Several months later, Billy, a three-month-old kitten was adopted for Katie.

"Joe-Willie White Shoes is in heaven since his friend Coop moved in," Willie's person reported. Willie was a year old when Coop, the same age, moved in. Because Willie and Coop both have mellow temperaments, they were a perfect match.

Companionship can make ideal patients out of the most difficult cats.

"Prissy's the model patient now that she has Rhett. She's no longer tense and actually appreciates contact," her people bragged. Before Rhett arrived in her life, she had chronic skin problems and every visit to the vet was upsetting to her.

Adopting an Older Cat for a Kitten

If you're adopting a mature cat for your kitten, the older cat, even though it's the newcomer, should be treated with partiality. You should treat your kitten as the newcomer because kittens are more adaptable in new situations.

Mary Astor, a one-year-old spayed cat, was adopted for Chicklet, a young kitten. Chicklet's person Renee followed the outlined procedure for introducing Mary but continued to give most of her attention to Chicklet. A few days later she called to say Mary and Chicklet just weren't getting along and that Chicklet spent most of her time hiding. I explained to Renee that Mary needed more support. It was important that she go out of her way to make Mary feel special and to refer to Chicklet as Mary's kitten. Because she already had a relationship with Chicklet, there was no way she could ignore her except to really concentrate on Mary. Renee was afraid Chicklet would become even more withdrawn, but I assured her that as soon as Mary felt secure and wanted to reach out to Chicklet she would do so. As long as Mary felt uneasy, she would give Chicklet a hard time. By the end of the week Renee reported that Mary and Chicklet were an item. The best part was that Chicklet would have Mary accompany her on jaunts in the garden.

Sometimes getting a relationship off to the wrong start has ended in its complete failure. One couple adopted a kitten for their cat with every good intention. They didn't know there was any particular way to go about it and managed unknowingly to do all they could to alienate their cat. The situation became so unbearable that they had to find another home for the kitten. Shortly after, they adopted another kitten and followed my step-by-step instructions. Finally, success! Their cat now has his very own friend.

Sylvester's experience is another one that could have been easier if his people hadn't complicated matters. Sylvester is a seven-year-old, declawed, altered cat who since kittenhood has been shy and stand-offish. His first home didn't work out because the people's older cat wouldn't accept him. Now seven years later he was presented with Flopsy, a three-month-old kitten whom Sylvester's people could not and would not ignore. They couldn't understand why Sylvester was rejecting Flopsy when they thought they were giving him all the encouragement and support he needed. Even his appetite had fallen off. They didn't realize that their patting and comforting Flopsy was the worst offense.

Finally, they concentrated on Sylvester and stopped worrying about Flopsy. Flopsy was forced to seek all her attention from Sylvester. She was not offended if Sylvester tried to ignore her; she only tried harder, and he finally had to give her the recognition she wanted. She even started washing his face. When Sylvester had enough, he would dismiss her with a bat of his paw. Unlike Sylvester, Flopsy is adventurous and not intimidated by new people or situations. He and Flopsy have a tolerable relationship but it could have been better. Fortunately, his people were able to change their behavior toward Flopsy. If they hadn't, she might have lost her home as Sylvester once did.

One client thought that her three-year-old cat, Snowball, might hurt a kitten instead of befriending it because of his tough personality. Snowball had been insecure since kittenhood. It took him months before he actually felt brave enough to explore the entire house, and even after that he usually retreated to the room he first started out in. He was affectionate with people only after he had met them several times. Sudden noises would cause him to run and hide.

Snowball used to go outdoors, but he was an absolute terror with any cat that crossed his path. With people he was shy and reticent. With other cats he was incorrigible.

I explained to Snowball's person that under normal circumstances an older cat would never hurt a kitten. This code does not apply to a street tom, who, because of his survival instinct, wouldn't hesitate to attack a kitten who was a threat to his food or territory. Another exception would be a mother cat who might kill one of her kittens if she felt it was sick or might endanger her other kittens.

Once Snowball's person was assured that a kitten would only help him to become more secure and outgoing, she decided to adopt one. It wasn't an easy experience for her because Snowball did all he possibly could to ignore and reject the kitten. His person almost literally had to sit on her hands to keep from petting the kitten because Snowball was so aloof. With the help of small doses of Valium to relieve his anxiety and with the love and support of Snowball's person, soon Snowball was touching noses with his kitten. The turning point came when Snowball washed her ear. From then on their relationship blossomed.

Adopting a Grown Cat for Your Mature Cat

It is important to remember that the adjustment will be longer for a grown cat–mature cat relationship—especially if your cat is shy or set in his ways.

Sammy is a two-year-old shy cat whose people decided that he needed his own friend. They adopted a two-year-old spayed female named Charli whose previous home was less than desirable. They followed my outlined procedure, but still each day was a major trauma for Sammy.

He was completely intimidated by Charli and his person had to literally carry him to the litter box and set up a special shelf for him to camp out on. Soon Sammy's confidence grew and Charli became less threatening. Because of the determination and support of Sammy's people, Sammy accepted Charli and she helped him to become more outgoing and sure of himself.

Priscilla is a six-year-old cat whose person decided that Priscilla needed her own friend to interact with each day. She decided to adopt Ring, an eighteen-year-old neutered male who had lived with a female cat before. For the first few days Priscilla's hostility kept Ring crouched under the bed. Because she wouldn't share her litter box, he accidentally used the velvet couch instead. His person had to set up Ring's own litter box and food close by her bed. When she found out that she had to go on an out-of-town business trip for a few days, she was skeptical about leaving them alone.

I advised her to arrange for a cat-sitter to come in twice a day and told her that their relationship would come together much quicker without her being there. Her anxiety and trepidation only increased Priscilla's hostility toward Ring.

When she returned home from her trip, she was amazed to find that Priscilla allowed Ring to venture freely throughout the whole apartment, and later she even shared the couch with him in front of the cozy fireplace.

Finding the right companion for your cat will go smoothly as long as you consider your cat's needs and heed the special step-by-step procedure I've explained. You must keep in mind that any relationship takes time to develop and you can't expect to have your cat greet his new companion with open arms. Sometimes a cat is so lonely and in such desperate need of companionship that he will immediately accept a newcomer, especially if he has been pining for a lost or deceased companion. However, normally you should plan on a couple of weeks for adjustment. Think back to the changes you had to make in your life when you first got your cat. For all this time, it's been just the two of you, but now you'll both have to adapt to living with the newcomer. If you really want the relationship to work you must realize that there might be a few upsets. But your cat will soon have his very own friend and you'll have two cats to love.

Chapter 4

Unneutered
Cats

Your first cat is neutered and now your second one has reached sexual maturity, but you just can't decide whether to have her spayed. She's had only a couple of heats, they didn't last long, she's so delicate, and your male cat didn't seem disturbed by them. You're thinking maybe you won't have to bother having her spayed. Avoiding the operation will be easier on both of you, you tell yourself.

Such thinking is erroneous. An unneutered cat is frequently neither healthy nor happy. Unless a female cat is constantly breeding, she won't ovulate. Soon the follicles in her ovaries become cystic. The resulting hormone imbalance makes her susceptible to both physical and personality disorders. Often an unspayed female forgets her toilet training and will not use her litter box.

Rinky, a three-year-old unspayed Manx, had always been fastidious about using her litter box. Suddenly, her heats were more frequent, she avoided her litter box, and often the smell of her urine was stronger. Soon her person noticed blood in her urine and took her to be examined.

Her urinalysis revealed she had a case of cystitis, which had to be treated. The vet recommended that Rinky be spayed. Surgery revealed a cyst on her ovary and an abnormally large uterus. Within two weeks after her surgery, she resumed her fastidious toilet habits. Her person was pleased at no longer finding unwanted specimens.

Personality disorders can manifest themselves as aggressive and hostile behavior toward people.

Ginger is a seven-year-old cat who used to attack Diane, one of the children in the family she lives with. Diane is very high-strung and timid. Her insecurity was enough to threaten Ginger, who was then unspayed and in a constant state of anxiety herself. Diane's insecurity triggered Ginger's anxiety, and her way of coping was to attack the source that was making her anxious—Diane. Ginger's people were frantic. They strongly considered giving Ginger up because they'd done all they could to keep Ginger away from Diane. All Ginger had to do was hear Diane's voice and she would start to hiss.

Ginger was spayed, then started on sedation, and finally presented with an adopted kitten. Her aggressive behavior disappeared and she no longer suffered the anxiety that caused her to attack in order to protect herself. She was now secure enough to cope with the high level of energy that Diane released.

Samantha is a three-year-old cat that would attack her person's girlfriends. She could not tolerate her person sharing his attention with any other female. It wasn't until she was spayed and presented with an adopted male kitten that her aggressive behavior stopped. Before Samantha was spayed, she was charged with a high degree of energy which, because she wasn't breeding, lay dormant and would frequently be triggered by anything that upset her and, as with her person's girlfriends, used destructively.

Her surgery relieved her of the mischanneling of this energy. A kitten provided her with a companion other than her person—one that she could relate to on a cat-to-cat basis.

Many times an intact female will suddenly become hostile and aggressive toward her companion cat.

Katie is a five-year-old cat who lives with her person and companion cat, Eloise. Eloise was spayed when she reached sexual maturity because her heats were frequent and severe. Because Katie's heats were infrequent, her person did not have her spayed at that time. Katie's relationship with Eloise had always been close. They slept together and washed each other. Suddenly one day Katie attacked without any apparent provocation. Two weeks later when the incident was repeated, Katie's person realized that Katie was in heat and had her spayed. However, Katie's behavior toward Eloise did not improve when she returned home from the hospital.

As I went over Katie's case with her person, it became apparent that anxiety was triggering Katie's attacks. Her first incident occurred when her person had a temper tantrum, and evidently Katie could not cope with the stress and took out her aggression on Eloise. Because she was unspayed for so long, she was very vulnerable to anxiety— especially when she was in heat. Until the first incident she was able to internalize her anxiety. I explained to Katie's person that having Katie spayed was the best thing she could have done. The important thing now was to relieve Katie of her anxiety so she would stop being hostile to Eloise. Even though she was spayed, it would take a while for her to reverse her behavior toward Eloise because she'd been anxiety ridden for so long.

Treatment consisted of starting both Katie and Eloise on sedation. I explained to Katie's person that Katie needed sedation to relieve her anxiety and Eloise needed sedation so that she wouldn't anticipate being attacked by Katie. Eloise's uneasiness would only add to Katie's anxiety. I told Katie's person it would be necessary to keep them separate until they had adapted to the sedation. When they both appeared relaxed, she could open the door and allow them to mingle. However, she shouldn't try to force them together, but let them interact at their own speed. Sedation was Katie's auxiliary support, but her primary support should consist of reassurance, frequent contact, and giving both cats a more nutritious diet (removing tuna from their diet).

A few days later Katie's person reported that Katie was off to a good start. She was more tolerant of Eloise and was even sleeping with her. Outwardly, Katie appeared happier and more relaxed. Their person had already started to change their diet *slowly* and both cats were not resistant. Eloise reacted favorably to the catnip but Katie became too excited. I explained that occasionally catnip could cause this reaction, but usually it caused a cat to become excited and active only for a short period of time and then to relax after releasing the energy. Evidently, Katie was still not emotionally integrated enough to handle the initial excitement. In a while Katie's stress tolerance would increase to the point where she could cope without the support of sedation and at that time, if not before, Eloise would no longer have the need for sedation. I pointed out to Katie's person that her love and understanding of her two cats could only hasten Katie's recovery. An occasional setback might have to be tolerated.

Sometimes the presence of an intact female can trigger hostile energy from a companion cat.

Patti, a five-year-old unspayed Siamese, lives with her litter mate Dugan, a neutered male, and an older neutered female, Izzy. The three of them were a loving circle, their person explained, except for the times when Patti went into heat and Dugan would grab her by the neck. Patti's heats were always brief and she never appeared uncomfortable. Then she started leaving noticeable urine stains around the apartment and there was frequently a potent smell after she urinated.

Other than Patti's toilet habits, the interaction of the three cats was stable. Then one evening their person entertained a woman guest whose voice was very piercing. Dugan was often uneasy around high female voices. Later that evening, he viciously attacked Izzy and was driven off by several buckets of water. Following this episode, both Patti and Dugan victimized Izzy.

I explained to their person that the sexual energy released by Patti in combination with the high energy released from the female visitor triggered Dugan's hostile behavior. However, he directed his aggression toward Izzy even though she was not the source of his anxiety.

As long as Patti was unspayed, Dugan's hostile behavior would continue. Patti's person realized the importance of having her spayed immediately, and she was scheduled for surgery. Her veterinarian found both her ovaries cystic and her uterus grossly enlarged. He commented that the surgery was performed none too soon. In a matter of months it could have progressed to a pyometra, a severe uterine infection that can be debilitating and sometimes fatal.

I explained that it would take about two weeks for Patti's hormones as well as her sexual tension to dissipate. Consequently, she would still be a source of anxiety to Dugan. Therefore, it was necessary to sedate all three cats.

Patti needed sedation so she would remain tranquil and not attempt to victimize Izzy. Izzy needed the support of sedation to relieve her constant state of anticipating an attack. Dugan needed sedation until his stress tolerance increased to the point where he was not obsessed with attacking Izzy. His sedation therapy was longer and greater than that of the females. Gradually, his doses were reduced and then stopped.

Sometimes the physical and emotional stress created by the hormonal imbalance can be fatal.

Circle was a three-year-old unspayed cat whose people didn't feel she had to be spayed because of her mild and infrequent heats. It wasn't until she developed lumps on her breast that they became concerned about her health.

Unfortunately, a biopsy revealed Circle had cancerous breast tumors. Because her emotional and physical state was adversely affected by her hormonal imbalance, she was a perfect target for cancer. We were able to keep her going for a while on drugs and supportive behavioral therapy, but her remaining time with her family lasted only several months. Some cats are able to go on longer in comfort but others don't make it as long as Circle. Often surgery can allay the cancer but, again, it's only a matter of time. Considering the alternatives, it's best to protect a female cat from unnecessary stress by having her spayed. Even though a female cat may not externalize her heats, she will internalize her discomfort and anxiety. As time goes on, the emotional stress that was triggered by the physical problem leaves her a perfect victim for cancer, which can be precipitated by emotional anxiety. An unspayed cat may not develop cancer but her chances of doing so are greater. Why gamble when there's a better solution?

An unaltered male, or tomcat, is in a constant state of stress. If he's an outdoor cat, he must constantly cope with other toms in territorial brawls and the conquering of female cats in heat. Often the tom is covered with scars, and a missing eye is not unusual. He's frequently hit by a car while on the run. The older a tom gets, the smaller his chances of winning and the greater his chances of getting severely injured by another tom.

Inky was a two-year-old tom with torn ears and a body covered with battle scars. His person was reluctant to alter Inky because he was afraid of ruining Inky's fun. Unconsciously, he identified with Inky and couldn't keep his emotions separate. It wasn't until Inky developed a severe respiratory problem and a lacerated eye from a brawl that his person decided to have him neutered.

Shortly after Inky's surgery, his person reported that Inky still roamed his turf but no longer brawled. He was amazed that Inky's personality hadn't changed, he was more relaxed, and his coat was beginning to shine.

Indoor tomcats sometimes manifest their stress through hostile and aggressive actions toward people.

Tiger was always a high-strung cat and often played hard and rough with his companion cat. He reached sexual maturity at seven months. His people weren't planning to have him altered because his urine wasn't especially strong smelling and their other cat was a spayed female. It wasn't until Tiger started spraying around the apartment, which is a tom's way of marking territory, that they became concerned. Then he would suddenly attack them by biting them on their legs and arms.

I explained to his people that Tiger's sexual maturity had triggered his aggressive behavior. Because he couldn't release his sexual energy by mating with unaltered female cats, his people became the target whenever he was stimulated or excited.

There is a surgical procedure called a vasectomy which is an alternative to castration.

Pyewacket, a one-year-old tom, lived with three college students. He was a tough and huskily built cat who didn't mind letting you sample his strength. He spent most of his time outdoors. His people didn't want him impregnating the neighborhood females but couldn't bring themselves to have Pyewacket altered. They decided on a vasectomy because they felt he would still be able to carry on his tomcatting without fathering any kittens.

Several weeks after the surgery they were quite confused by its effects. They hadn't realized that the vasectomy would not prevent Pyewacket from spraying and they thought he might be doing it out of spite or perhaps because he had cystitis. Pyewacket was perfectly healthy and his behavior was not spiteful. Unlike a castration, in which the testicles are removed, a vasectomy entails severing the tube that carries sperm from the testes. This prevents conception but doesn't rid a cat of the hormones which enable it to spray.

Pyewacket's treatment was castration. Two weeks later he stopped spraying and his people felt they had finally made the best decision for him.

Sometimes a male cat will continue to spray long after he has been altered. When this happens, generally there is something major wrong. Although it is true that an altered male cat is able to spray, it is rare that he will; and even then, the odor is not strong like that of a tomcat.

Rusty, a two-year-old male, was altered just before his people adopted him from a local shelter. They were told that he might spray for a couple of weeks but then he would stop. A couple of months passed and still he continued to spray. They were able to cope with an occasional incident, but it became a daily ritual.

They brought him to me because they were desperate and even talked of giving Rusty up. They explained that Rusty backed up against an object, jerked his tail in the air, and sprayed. The smell was unbearable, they added. It was then that I realized what Rusty's problem was. I told them that when Rusty was altered only one of his testicles was removed. Rusty was acting like a tomcat because he was one! I recommended that they make an appointment with their vet to perform an exploratory operation and have the testicle removed.

Leaving a supposedly castrated cat with an intact testicle was gross negligence on the part of the initial veterinarian, but it does happen. The veterinarian routinely removes the descended testicle but does not take the time to find the one that has not descended. He may feel incapable of performing this more-involved surgery; however, it's his duty to inform the client that the cat is likely to exhibit tomcat symptoms if the surgery isn't performed.

There are common misconceptions about the behavior of neutered cats. The following information will correct some of these unfortunate myths:

1. Neutered males and females do not lose their sensuality after they're altered. This happens only if they are neutered before reaching full sexual maturity. A female cat usually reaches sexual maturity between five-and-a-half and eleven months of age. She should be spayed after her first heat. A male cat usually reaches sexual maturity between six and twelve months. You can tell that he's ready to be altered when he becomes more aggressive, prowls and cries at the door, and his urine develops a distinctive pungent odor.

2. Unlike people, cats cannot intellectualize their sexuality. They react on emotional and sensual levels. They experience sensations by feeling, not by thinking things out. Cats are not rational. Their senses, which are finely developed, control their behavior.

3. Neutered cats do not automatically become fat and lazy. They do become more relaxed, and if they are indoor cats and their diet isn't controlled they will tend to be overweight.

When cats reach sexual maturity, the hormone levels trigger an area in the brain that, from that time on, controls their femininity or masculinity. After they're neutered, these characteristics are neurally controlled without the need of further hormone stimulation. Therefore, once maturity is reached, a cat's sexuality is not dependent on his or her sexual organs. He or she has already achieved the ultimate state of differentiation.

Unneutered cats are more prone to urinary and skin problems because they're under constant stress.

Patches was a two-year-old altered male and his companion cat was Sandy, a nine-month-old female. Sandy had several heats after she was seven months old. At first Patches wasn't affected, didn't seem to notice, their person explained. But now, Patches was urinating indiscriminately and Sandy was tearing away at her skin.

I recommended that they both be examined by their veterinarian and that Sandy be spayed. Evidently, the discomfort and stress she experienced each time she had a heat caused her to tear away at her skin. Her skin became her target. Sandy's sexual tension triggered Patches' urinary problem. His bladder became the target for his frustration. Once Sandy was spayed, the source of anxiety for both of them would be removed and their secondary problems would gradually disappear. Until then, they would each have to be treated medically for their ailments.

So far, your female may not have experienced any of these problems. But she has a good number of years to live and a good many heats to experience. To insure her health, your peace of mind, and your male cat's comfort, you should make an appointment to have her spayed.

49

Chapter 5

Professional
Services

You've decided to have your female cat spayed. Now all that you have to do is call and make the appointment with your vet. But you're still a bit hesitant about taking the final step. It has nothing to do with your vet. She's terrific! It's your cat you're worried about. She was impossible the last time you brought her in. All the vet had to do was vaccinate her, but your cat managed to hiss and scream through the whole appointment. By the time you reached home she had both urinated and defecated in her carrier. Her fur was all matted and smelly.

The hysteria didn't end there. Your male cat treated her as the enemy and even attacked her a few times. It wasn't until the next day that they were on friendly terms again. If getting her spayed means another experience like the last, you're wondering if it's worth it.

There is a way that you can make a trip to the vet's office a calmer experience for everyone concerned. Your female becomes hysterical when she goes to the vet because she is anxious. Her aggressive behavior is actually self-defense. Many cats react this way when they are frightened. To prevent her from becoming anxious, it would be best to sedate her before taking her to the vet. Have your vet recommend a tranquilizer, but try it out before you schedule her appointment so that you're sure it will be effective. If it isn't, your vet may increase or decrease the dosage or suggest another tranquilizer. Whether or not she needs a tranquilizer, proceed with the following instructions:

1. Don't feed her for at least three hours before her appointment. It's best to keep her stomach empty so that it doesn't get upset.

2. Take out her cat carrier, fill it with strips of newspaper, and sprinkle catnip inside. The catnip is to make the carrier inviting to her.

3. Encourage your male cat to play in the carrier so it has his familiar smell. You might even give them treats in the carrier if the catnip doesn't entice them.

4. When it comes time to leave, put her in the carrier with a few reassuring strokes and squeezes. If she protests going into the carrier, cup your hands over her eyes as you put her in so she doesn't see. Be sure to tell her she'll be home soon and her companion will be waiting for her. Reassure him too. (Neither will understand your words but they will benefit from your feeling.)

5. Put a toy with your male cat's smell in the carrier with her.

Arrival at the Vet's Office

1. Keep the carrier next to you so that she feels your presence.

2. Try to keep her away from other patients so that she doesn't become more excited. *Don't* attempt to introduce her to other cats.

3. If the waiting room is empty or if she won't be aware of other patients, open the carrier and give her a few pets and hugs.

4. Whatever you do, don't let her out of her carrier. This will only add to her nervousness.

5. During her appointment, give her words of reassurance. Try to remain calm so that you don't transfer your nervousness to her.

6. Don't stare at the needle if the vet has to give her an injection or administer any kind of uncomfortable treatment. Place all your concentration on her and try to distract her. This way you'll both be less aware of the treatment.

7. If you're permitted to accompany her to where she's being admitted, assure her you'll return to visit her. Don't forget to leave your male cat's toy with her, and take home some of the strips of newspaper from her carrier for him to smell. (If you're not able to accompany her to the hospital area, you can do this in the examining room.) Make sure you know when your vet will be in contact with you after her surgery and when you can pick her up.

8. If visiting is permitted, arrange a time to visit her. Visiting does wonders for a patient.

When you arrive home, don't forget to give your male cat the strips of paper from her carrier. Give him lots of hugs and tell him that his girlfriend will be home soon.

She hasn't run off and left him. Reward him with something good to eat, and maybe fix a drink for yourself. He may start searching for her and even begin to cry. If he does, hug him tightly and breathe deeply yourself.

When you pick her up after her surgery, she may not give you a cordial reception. After all, as far as she's concerned, you did go off and leave her. If she acts aloof, never mind. Go right ahead and give her much love and encouragement. She may even be testing you to see how much you really do care about her. Remind her that her boyfriend is home waiting for her and repeat how much you've both missed her.

Arrival Home from the Vet

1. Open the carrier and let her out.

2. Sprinkle some fresh catnip in the carrier to encourage your male cat to jump in.

3. By going inside the carrier, soon he'll pick up her smell and she won't smell unfamiliar to him. Otherwise he may find her hospital smell threatening and treat her aggressively.

4. There may be some hissing from both sides or they may ignore each other for awhile. Relax, and soon they'll be back to normal.

Soon her sutures will be removed, the fur that was shaved for the incision will grow back, and spaying your female will be just another memory.

If you have a long-haired cat, she can be groomed while under anesthesia for the spaying. Many people find grooming a long-haired cat an ordeal. It's the tangles on her tummy you always have difficulty with. You should try to comb her every day, but if you've been remiss in the past couple of weeks her tangles may have become un-bearable. If you simply don't have the time or the energy to groom her yourself, a professional groomer is your answer.

Try to make an appointment with one who will groom her in your own home. Why subject her to a strange place where she might pick up infections from other cats? Grooming will be more comfortable and less stressful if your cat can stay where she feels safe and protected. Make her grooming experience a pleasant one.

You may find it inconvenient to be constantly carting home cat food and litter. Perhaps you've thought of cook-ing for your cats, but you don't even cook for yourself.

You'll be pleased to know that there are many pet-food supply outlets where you can purchase food and litter in quantity. Many of these suppliers deliver right to your door. The main advantage is that because you're buying in quantity it's less expensive. Check your phone book for nearby locations.

Ever since your male cat took an unannounced cruise from your apartment, you worry about your cats becoming lost. Especially now that you've been letting them out in the garden there's a definite risk. They do have safety collars with identifications but you're still skeptical.

If you want permanent identity for your cats, check into a service called Ident-A-Pet that will tattoo a number on the inside of your cat's ear. They also provide your cat with an identification tag that has the number on it, says that your cat is protected by Ident-A-Pet, and gives the phone number to call. Ident-A-Pet's headquarters is in New Jersey but it provides a national service. Their fee is about twenty dollars and their phone number is 800-526-4251, a toll-free call.

If you're fortunate, your cats have an idyllic relationship and, except for an occasional problem, you have no com-plaints about their behavior. It's unlikely you'll ever have to consult a behavioral therapist for your cat. However, it would be beneficial for you to be acquainted with a behaviorist's function.

Unlike a veterinarian, a cat therapist does not treat your cat's medical problems. Instead, he or she deals with your cat's behavior and emotions. If the therapist feels your cat's problem is actually medical, he or she will recommend that your cat be checked by your veterinarian.

When clients make an appointment to see me, they are told to bring their cat with them. It is important that their cat be present for the consultation so that I can get a feeling of what he's like. If the client has younger children, I recommend that they don't come along. There is usually a pull from the child for the client's attention. It is essential that the cat receive all the attention.

Unless the cat will sit calmly in the person's lap, he remains in the carrier but in a central spot where our attention is focused on him. I always sprinkle some catnip into the carrier. By the end of the consultation, the cat is usually more relaxed than when he arrived. The catnip may be partially responsible for this reaction, but the primary reason is that our conversation has been limited to the cat. True, he cannot follow our words, but he can feel that our concentration is on him and it makes him feel good. After listening to the cat's case history and asking pertinent questions, I write down my impressions and treatment plan. Then I discuss it with the client and write down the treatment plan and instructions for him. If the cat needs any type of sedation, my associate, Dr. Rowan, who is a veterinarian, is able to write a prescription. After the initial consultation, most of the contact is done by phone. Occasionally, I will request to see the patient again. It's up to the client to keep me informed of the patient's progress, and the more conscientious the client, the better the prognosis.

There are other professional services offered for cats, such as cat hotels and pet shops, which I do not recommend. Most of these operations are strictly profit oriented and the individual cat is not considered. Also, there's a strong potential for exposure to infectious disease. I have chosen to deal only with the essential professional services that will benefit your cats.

Chapter 6

The Declawed Cat

Up until last week, it really didn't bother you that your cats scratched away at your living-room carpet and ran their claws across your tattered sofa. But now you're concerned! You've decided to redecorate and you've ordered a new wall-to-wall carpet, a velvet sofa, and a matching armchair. You'll simply die if your cats treat your new things like the old. Occasionally you clip their claws and they do have a scratching post, but it fell down on one of them once and they never used it again.

A couple of your friends have had their cats declawed. You don't have a good feeling about declawing but your friends' cats seem okay. It would be great not to worry about their tearing up your new things. Maybe it would be best to have them declawed. Then you know there would be no chance of your getting mad at them for carrying on a destruction derby.

If your friends' cats didn't suffer any postoperative problems from being declawed they were fortunate.

Simply and finally, get the idea of having your cats' claws removed out of your head! A cat is born with claws because he needs them. Tearing out a cat's claws is similar to removing our fingernails, and you might say that our fingernails are less essential to our well-being than a cat's claws are to his. A cat needs his claws for grasping things, for hunting and climbing if he's outdoors, and for self-defense. Without claws, a cat's balance is not as good as it should be and many declawed cats fall from open windows. A cat's claws are retractable and are not spread out all the time.

Removing a cat's claws is unnatural and unhealthy. The surgery is risky and the recovery is slow and painful. Generally, the operation is as follows:

1. Your cat is given a general anesthetic.

2. The fur around the feet is clipped.

3. A tourniquet is placed around the leg.

4. The nails are rinsed with alcohol.

5. The nails' amputation is done with a guillotine nail-cutter, which cuts across the first joint and often includes the foot pad.

6. To prevent hemorrhage, the toes are bandaged.

7. The bandage is removed two to three days after the operation.

8. In an alternate procedure, the nail is removed completely and the skin is sutured over. Because it's more time consuming, this procedure is not as common.
Physical complications are numerous:

1. There may be an adverse reaction to general anesthetic.

2. Tight bandages can cause gangrene in the foot and may require amputation of the leg.

3. When bandages are removed there may be hemorrhaging, which requires rebandaging.

4. If the entire nail bed isn't removed, claws can later begin to regrow; but they'll regrow misshapen and useless.

5. Infection and drainage may develop that can be corrected only by a second general anesthetic and surgical procedure.

Wonka is a five-year-old cat who was declawed last year. Since then she's needed two further operations. Her nails had shattered, causing recurrent infection. Now she has to undergo yet another operation. An abscess has developed where her right dew claw was, and it extends down to the bone. If it isn't reopened, it will continue to reinfect and constantly drain. It's been a traumatic period for Wonka but she still remains gentle and trusting.

Some cats have not been so lucky. The emotional stress suffered from declawing has triggered severe physical disorders, such as chronic cystitis, dermatitis, and asthma.

Claws are essential to a cat's physical and emotional development. Declawing causes definite emotional complications:

1. The cat is disoriented because of throbbing and bandaged feet.

2. After the bandages are removed, the cat is frustrated

over the absence of its claws and uncomfortable because it hurts to walk.

3. The cat is confused because its balance is affected.

When a declawed cat is severely stressed by these complications, he becomes anxious. Anxiety is a chief precipitating factor in asthma and other physical diseases. A declawed cat is a prime target for physical complications.

Claws are a cat's first line of defense against threat. Because he can't scratch, a declawed cat is more apt to bite when threatened. Frequently, a declawed cat becomes distrustful of his person because he feels inadequate and insecure. This is especially so in new or tense situations, because he knows he can't strike out if upset.

Some people brag that their cat can't hurt you because he has no front claws. He still has his teeth, and a cat bite can do more damage than a scratch.

A declawed cat often becomes hysterical when he has to be examined by a veterinarian. He has a built-in source of fear resulting from his painful surgery. There is no reason for him to feel any trust. To compensate for his insecurity, he will often try to bite in self-defense. There is every reason for him to feel tense and uncomfortable.

Many people wonder why their declawed cat will suddenly give them a chomp on the ankle or a nip on the wrist. He would use his front claws, *if* he had any, as a means of attracting their attention. However, he can't scratch so he resorts to a bite. I've often thought these people are getting off easy compared to what their cats have experienced when they were declawed.

It's not unusual for part of a cat's foot pad to be accidentally removed along with the nails. This may often pose serious postoperative problems.

Angel's claws were removed and after surgery he walked with his front paws partially tucked under. His person couldn't understand why he walked this way.

Part of Angel's foot pads were cut off when he was declawed and this error deformed his feet, causing his curled-under stance.

Angel's person had him declawed because the operation had been done to her other cat. Like many other people, she didn't know that a cat with claws won't take advantage of his declawed friend. When it comes to wrestling or playing with each other, the declawed cat will nip when he's had enough roughhousing from the other.

Yes, it is important for you to protect your new possessions, but the well-being of your cats comes first. The best solution is a good sturdy scratching post covered with strong material and filled with catnip. If you can't make an adequate one, it can be purchased from Felix Catnip Tree Co., 416 Smith Street, P.O. Box 9594, Seattle, Washington, 98109. If your cats have a post worthy of their scratching, one that won't attack them when they attempt to scratch it, they will use it. Don't have their claws removed and regret it for the rest of your life.

Chapter 7

Traveling with Your Cat

These past few years have been rough for you but it's all been worth it. You now have three weeks of paid vacation and you've decided to rent a house at the seashore. The best part is that you'll be able to go there on the weekends even after you return to work. You know the situation will be ideal for you but you're wondering how your cats will react to a whole new environment. Until now, you've only taken them on small excursions in the car, during which they screamed most of the way. You're wondering if there's a way to go about this with a minimal amount of discomfort.

There are certain provisions that you can make for the trip and for after your arrival that will make the journey a relatively painless ordeal.

If the trip is long (four or more hours), your cats may need sedation. You can use oral or injectable medication. Check with your veterinarian. If you decide on the oral type, be sure to give your cats a trial dosage beforehand to

make sure it will be effective. (If your cats have nervous or queasy stomachs, Dramamine is often advisable.) An injectable sedation is generally more reliable. If your cats will be going outdoors, check with your veterinarian to see if a rabies vaccination is necessary for that area. It's also best to have your cats vaccinated against respiratory viruses and make sure their distemper boosters are current.

Do not feed your cats for at least four hours before departure. An empty stomach is better than an upset one.

Supplies for the Trip

1. Disposable cardboard litter box or plastic pan and plastic litter-box liners, which can be purchased in most pet-supply departments of supermarkets, dime stores, and department stores.

2. Scooper and litter.

3. Food, bowls, and catnip.

4. Favorite toy, scratching post.

5. Carrier. It should be lined with strips of newspaper in case your cat has an accident. The kind with the wire top is best because it allows air to circulate freely. The carrier should have your identification on the outside.

Auto Trip

1. Set up the litter box in a convenient area of car.

2. Try to have the car as cool as possible.

3. If your cats decide to hide when it comes time to carry them to the car in their carrier, relax, breathe deeply, and entice them with catnip or a tiny food treat.

4. If you decide to let them out of the carrier in the car, leave the windows open only a crack. Some cats prefer to stay inside the carrier because they feel protected. The noise of the traffic, motion of the car, and wide open spaces can frighten them. You might compare it to your first experience in an airport or bus terminal.

5. If you must leave them alone in the car for awhile and it's a hot day, park in a shady spot and leave the windows open a crack. Don't take a chance on having your cat become a victim of heat prostration. The inside temperature can often be hotter than you realize. On a clear sunny day when the outside temperature is 80 degrees, the temperature in a closed car can easily reach 120 degrees.

Upon reaching your holiday destination, the following will make the arrival less traumatic:

1. Set up the litter box and water bowl in the bathroom.

2. Bring the carrier inside and close the bathroom door.

3. Open the carrier so that your cats can venture out to explore the litter box and bathroom.

4. The carrier should remain open awhile so that your cats have a nearby familiar object containing their scent.

5. Talk to them softly, stroke them, and hug them tightly if they're anxious.

6. After they become familiar with the bathroom, they're ready to explore the rest of the house.

7. If your house is large, try to arrange it so they can explore one room at a time. Otherwise, the newness and vastness may overwhelm them.

8. You can give them some catnip and offer them a light meal three to four hours after arrival.

Don't be startled if your cats talk constantly or even hide upon reaching the destination. If they've been tranquilized, this behavior may not occur right away, but it could the following day. It will take a few days for your cats to adapt to their new environment.

If you plan to allow them to go outdoors, take the following precautions:

1. Make sure your cats are completely familiar and secure with the inside of the house before you allow them to venture outdoors.

2. Provide them with collars and identification even if they are tattooed. They may also need a flea collar or medallion.

3. You may want to install a commercial kitty door.

4. At first, don't allow your cats to go out alone. Accompany them on short strolls around the house. Use kitty harnesses and leashes. It's important for them to first familiarize themselves under your supervision with the immediate area surrounding the house. Then when they're on their own, and if for any reason they panic, they'll know where they can go to hide and/or return quickly inside the house.

5. Don't permit your cats to stay out after dark.

6. Convince them to come home in the evening by feeding them at sundown.

Departure

1. When it's time to leave your vacation spot, don't feed your cats for at least four hours before departure.

2. Follow the same instructions as for the auto trip to the resort.

3. Make a checklist of their supplies that you want to take with you so you're sure you haven't forgotten anything.

4. Don't forget their sedation if it's necessary.

Upon arriving home, don't be surprised if your cats are at first disoriented, but it won't take them long to adapt to being back.

Once you start traveling with your cats, you'll be sorry if you have to leave them at home. You might find you want to take them hotel-hopping with you at some point. Many hotels permit cats in the rooms. (Follow the instructions for supplies for the auto trip. However, if you like to travel light, you may not be able to take along their scratching post.)

Upon Arriving at the Hotel

1. Tell the bellhop which bag has your cats if you don't have an easily identified carrier. It's best if you carry them yourself so they will feel more secure.

2. Talk to them calmly and softly if they start to cry.

3. The hotel may ask you to sign an agreement holding you responsible for any possible damage caused by your cats.

Refer to the instructions for arrival outlined in the "Auto Trip" section above. In addition, be sure to put up the "Do Not Disturb" sign whenever you leave your room. Otherwise, someone may enter and inadvertently let your cats out. Let your maid know your cats are along and ask her not to leave the door to your room ajar when she cleans.

Follow the instructions for departure outlined for the "Auto Trip." In addition, make sure you leave the room neat for the next cats.

One day you may even want to take your cats traveling to another state or to a foreign country.* Some states and most foreign countries require shots or vaccinations for cats before entry. Your vet may have a book, *State and Federal Health Requirements and Regulations*, published by the United States Department of Agriculture, listing domestic and Canadian requirements and any quarantines. The book is also available in some public libraries. If you are traveling to a foreign country, the respective embassy can provide you with the information you need for your cats' entry.

If you're traveling by air, airlines can supply you with information regarding foreign restrictions and necessary forms, but the consulate of the country you're traveling to would be the best source. Do your checking in advance so you're not suddenly disappointed. Hawaii and England have a quarantine and their governments will charge for boarding. Some islands in the Caribbean will not accept your cats at all.

Your cats will have to travel in a carrier. Various airlines have regulation carriers, usually made of plastic, that you may purchase from them. Once again, be sure to line the carrier with strips of newspaper and attach a label to it with complete identification, including your destination. Some airlines will allow at least one pet per cabin as long as the carrier will fit safely under the seat in front of you. (Since two cats can fit in the same carrier, it may be possible for both to ride in the cabin.) Try to make your

---

* Much of the following information was taken from Michael Norman, "A Guide for Owners of Pets in Transit," *New York Times Travel Section,* 26 June 1977.

reservation as soon as possible or your cats will have to travel as "excess baggage" in the cargo or luggage hold. Some airlines even have a limit on the number of animals in the cargo hold so, again, don't delay in making their reservation.

The following information will help make your trip easier:

1. Try to reserve a direct flight so there's no chance that your cats will be transferred to the wrong plane.

2. Try not to reserve a flight during weekends and holidays. The airline is more apt to be cordial about handling your cats if it's not pressured.

3. In warm weather, try to reserve a flight in early morning or after sundown.

4. Before leaving for the airport, call and ask them for a ground-condition report. Try to reschedule your flight if the temperature is 80 degrees or more at the airport and the humidity is high.

5. Arrive at the airport at least 45 minutes before takeoff.

6. If your cats are traveling in the baggage hold, don't allow the reservations clerk to put their carrier on the baggage conveyor belt.

7. Carry your carrier to the boarding area and have an airline employee personally see that your cats board the plane. Instruct the employee to delay boarding until no more than a half hour before takeoff.

8. Upon arrival at your destination, ask an airline employee to bring your cats to you. Avoid letting them sit waiting on a loading dock or in a concrete waiting room in inclement weather.

9. Avoid peak travel periods. The less baggage in the cargo compartment, the greater the "free-air volume," and that is highly significant. You can receive a complete explanation of this and general information about a baggage hold by writing for a booklet called "Safe Animal Transportation in Passenger Aircraft." It's published by the McDonnell Douglas Corporation, Douglas Aircraft Company, 3855 Lakewood Blvd., Long Beach, California, 90801.

No doubt you are aware of the casualties among animals that have been transported in the cargo holds of jet aircraft. Your cats are greatly affected by extremes in temperature, engine noises, and exhaust fumes even before they board the plane. If they become overheated or chilled or overly stressed, the cargo hold can only add to their discomfort—even if it is adequately equipped. Once your cats are aboard, they are affected by heat and humidity and restricted ventilation. The temperature and air flow in the baggage compartment of a big jet are controlled by the following factors:

1. The longer a jet sits on the ground loading or unloading in hot weather, the hotter the hold will be.

2. If the hold is overloaded with luggage, your cats' breathable air will be drastically cut down.

Heat prostration or hyperventilation can prove fatal to your cats.

If you get a bad or indifferent feeling from the ticket agents of an airline about your concern for your cats, check with the cargo manager. If there's still no satisfaction, try to fly with another airline.

If you decide to travel by railroad, your cats must travel in a carrier. Again, be sure the carrier is labeled with complete identification. Some smaller railroads allow your cats to accompany you into the car as long as they remain in their carrier. Cats can't travel on Metroliners and Amfleet and some short-haul trains not equipped with baggage cars. Other railroads such as Amtrak allow cats to travel only in the baggage car. When you call for a reservation, find out if the train has a baggage car and whether both your departure and arrival stations handle checked baggage. Amtrak's personnel will water your cats at station stops along the way. Passengers are allowed to feed and visit their cats at station stops lasting ten minutes or more. These would be good times to tidy and clean the inside of their carrier. Don't forget to pack enough food for the trip.

If you are traveling first class, you are not usually charged an excess baggage fee for your cats: If by coach, you are charged a rate based on the total weight of your cats and carrier.

Don't take your cats on a long train trip during cold weather in a northern climate. Most baggage cars are not heated and your cats may be affected. Also, try to avoid traveling in very hot weather.

Traveling with your cats by bus may be impossible. Most major interstate bus lines in the continental United States don't permit cats. Some intracity lines also bar cats. At other times, it may depend on the whim of the bus driver.

Whether you're traveling by plane or train, refer to the general information outlined above for traveling by car. You'll find that traveling with your cats can be as much fun as you make it. Certainly, your cats more than deserve a holiday along with you!

Chapter 8

Traveling Without Your Cat

Your cats are curled up together in their basket washing each other. This is a common sight but you never get tired of watching them. It makes you feel so good inside to know they give each other such pleasure. At moments like this you especially realize how much you love them.

You're trying to tell yourself that next month will never come or maybe you won't have to go. You've always wanted to go to London, but now that your company is sending you there for a month, all expenses paid, you're unhappy. If only London didn't quarantine animals, your cats could go with you. They had such a wonderful time at the seashore and it was so much fun having them along. You know London will be exciting but you'll be so lonely without your cats.

Up until yesterday your friend was going to stay at your home with them but she had to cancel out. Now you don't even know who to leave them with.

Since your cats can't travel with you, it's vital to their

physical and mental health that you make the proper provisions during your absence. While you're away, your cats are subject to extra emotional stress, which can easily trigger a physical problem. Even for a couple of days, it's not enough to leave an extra supply of food and kiss your cats goodbye.

Whatever you do, never board your cats. Cats are very vulnerable to sickness when they're kept near other cats. Their vulnerability increases when they're separated from their people and home. Any added emotional stress lowers their resistance and makes them an excellent target for stray virus or bacteria.

D. W. Griffith is a two-year-old cat who was boarded at a cat hotel while his person was away. When his person picked D. W. up, his eyes were running and he was sneezing. He returned home with a severe respiratory virus. His person vowed he'd never board D. W. again.

It's unnatural for healthy cats that are used to the care of their person and comforts of their home to find themselves suddenly in a cage or cubicle where they are aware of strange cats, noises, and scents. Not only is the experience disorienting to them, it is also depressing. Think of how hard it is for sick cats to suddenly be hospitalized.

If you can't arrange for a friend to stay with your cats, perhaps your cats can stay with a friend. It's the second-best choice. Don't forget to pack their favorite toys and don't exclude their scratching post: they'll be more prone to mischief in a strange place. Warn your friend that they may hide for a couple of days or their appetite may be off. However, if they stop eating or urinating completely for more than two days, they should be checked by their veterinarian. It will take them a while to adapt to a new environment, but if your friend really appreciates them, they'll soon be jumping into bed.

Raisin was a six-year-old cat whose person frequently went on short business trips. He usually arranged for someone to put out food for Raisin and care for him while he went away. But one time he departed and left Raisin with just dry food and no one to visit. Three days later Raisin's person returned to find Raisin listless and crouched in a corner. At first, he thought Raisin was just sulking because he'd been left alone. But when Raisin started to cry, he knew something was wrong and he'd better get Raisin off to the vet.

The vet found that Raisin's bladder was obstructed and he was unable to urinate. A catheter couldn't be inserted into the urethra and the vet had to tap Raisin's bladder. Only then was the vet able to pass the catheter. Raisin then had to be hospitalized for a week and full recovery took a month.

Going off and leaving your cats alone for a few days is inviting trouble. Because they are stressed, their resistance is low and they cannot function as well on a day-to-day basis. As with Raisin, if any problem starts and goes unnoticed for a few days, you may not be able to catch it in time. It might even be fatal.

If you're going to be away for only a couple of days, arrange for a friend to come in twice a day to feed and visit with your cats. Otherwise, arrange for a neighbor's child to come in. Another alternative is engaging a professional cat-sitter.

Remember to leave written instructions about your cats' diet, veterinarian, and chronic medical problems, if there are any. With certain medications, it's usually best to increase the dosage while you're away. Check with your veterinarian. Usually, your cat will need more support than a maintenance dosage because of the additional emotional stress. Don't forget to let the person know your cats' favorite games and the places where they're partial to being stroked or scratched. Remind the person not to leave any windows open from the bottom: if necessary, they can be cracked open from the top. Most important, leave the number of someone they can contact if for any reason they're unable to take care of your cats.

If your cats snub you when you return from your trip, keep working at regaining their purrs. After all, you did go away and leave them!

79

Chapter 9

There Must Be a Way

Time has again passed quickly. London was fun and productive but you're glad to be back home with your cats. For the first week they were rather standoffish with you but now they're their old cuddly selves. You really missed sleeping with them in London. Now you're one happy family again. The first few days you were back you didn't even get annoyed when they woke you up to feed them their breakfast. Of course, that bit of tolerance has passed but otherwise almost all is well.

What's bothering you now is that your female is looking very bedraggled and the groomer is on holiday. You're able to comb out her tangles but she dearly needs a bath. Her daily jaunts in the garden are often hard on her appearance. Yesterday she managed to get something sticky in her fur which you could barely comb out.

When the groomer bathed her, you never paid much attention to how she went about it. She didn't seem to have any problem but then she's a professional. You've just naturally put bathing your cat in the "hopeless" category.

Don't despair! There is a way that you can give your cat a bath with a minimum of stress. Let the following instructions be your guide:

Equipment

1. The kitchen sink, if it's large enough (if not, a tub).

2. Lighting: make sure it's adequate.

3. Baby shampoo and gentle rinse or conditioner.

4. Q-tips and baby oil.

5. Hair dryer.

6. Three large towels.

7. Three different-sized combs.

8. Scissors.

9. Waste receptacle.

10. Mercuric oxide ointment (this can be purchased at the drugstore).

11. Pot or basin to use for rinsing.

12. Newspaper to spread on floor around sink or tub.

Preparation

1. Clean your cat's ears with Q-tips immersed in baby oil.

2. Apply eye ointment to her eyes.

3. Pet and praise.

Procedure
Now your cat is ready for combing. Start with stomach area and underparts.

1. Separate large tangles into smaller ones. Pet and comfort as you work.

2. Work from the outer tip of the tangle in toward the skin.

3. When all tangles are separated and comb goes through hair freely, your cat is ready for the bath, almost.

Bathing

1. Make sure air temperature isn't too cold.

2. Fill pot or basin with tepid rinse water and set it to the side.

3. Place cat in sink or tub and hold by scruff of neck, firmly but gently.

4. Slowly fill basin with water. Wet her back and legs and belly thoroughly.

5. Apply shampoo and rub in. Use shampoo sparingly. The more you apply, the more you must rinse out.

6. Rinse with a basin or pot of tepid water, followed by water from tap, and then apply rinse or conditioner. Again, rinse thoroughly.

Drying

1. Take towel and wrap up your cat and rub vigorously. Hug and kiss as you rub.

2. Apply dryer while fluffing hair with comb. Continue until dry, pretty, and happy.

3. Clean combs, comb once more.

It's most important while you're grooming and bathing to keep up a running monologue that's soothing and reassuring. Your cat needs your constant support in order not to panic or become difficult. Try to think of good and happy thoughts so they will be transferred to your cat. It would be ideal if you could get a friend to help you, but make sure the friend is calm and relaxed. If your cat is nervous but responds well to tranquilizers, by all means, sedate. It's best to keep stress and anxiety to a minimum. When you're all finished and your cat simply shines, be sure to praise and praise.

It's a few days later and she still looks terrific. Only this afternoon was a horror show for you. Every Saturday afternoon, while you're catching up on your reading and enjoying a pot of tea inside, your cats are romping in the garden. Then at 6:00 you call them in for dinner. They'd been outside only a short time when your female appeared with a bird in her mouth. She dropped it down beside you and she almost seemed to be smiling. You were so upset you started to yell at her. She immediately ran under the sofa. At that point your male cat appeared and started batting the bird around. Frantically, you stamped your feet and he ran outside, dropping the bird. It took all the courage you could muster to wrap the bird in a towel and bury it in a secluded part of the garden. Your cats kept out of sight until dinner, and by that time you'd recovered from the afternoon's incident. You knew you shouldn't be mad at them but it was such a painful episode. You wonder if you could cope any better if it happened again.

First you must accept the fact that cats are natural hunters. Hunting is instinctive and not something they're conditioned to, such as having people provide them with food. Religiously, they bring their prey as love tokens to their special person. It's hard for many people to appreciate their gift. Scolding a cat only confuses and frustrates him. You're defying nature if you reprimand a cat for hunting. There is a way you can deal with it so it isn't such a painful experience. You might even be able to prevent it from happening:

1. If your cats go outdoors, you can attach a bell to their collars if birds are in the vicinity.

2. Don't feed birds if your cats go outdoors. You are only setting up an inevitable trap for the birds.

3. If your cat should present you with a dead bird, pet and praise him and try to look around the bird so you won't become upset.

4. Distract your cat with catnip, food, or cooked chicken parts.

5. If you have the feeling your cat wants to eat the bird, pick it up in tinfoil or a paper towel and put it outside for him. Chances are your cat will follow you to the spot and you won't have to direct him. There is a possibility that your cat will contract worms from eating birds. However, if you have your cat's stool checked every few months, your vet will be able to treat the problem.

6. Possibly, your cat will forget about the bird and you'll be able to bury it in your garden.

Animals in the wild always eat their prey. Domesticated cats still have the hunting instinct, but because their food is provided, their hunger may already be satiated, so they may not always eat their prey.

Often cats can be brought up with birds or hamsters that they won't harm and can live with in harmony. But this conditioned response is the exception rather than the rule. In some cats, a strong hunting instinct is hereditary, but there is usually no easy way to determine this.

By the end of the weekend you'd regained your good spirits and your cats were in your usual good graces. You even gave them special treats of Swiss cheese and melon.

Last week you took them to the vet for their annual checkup and booster vaccinations. The vet checked a stool sample, informed you that they had worms, and gave them each a pill. She told you you'd have to repeat the medication again, and tonight's the night. It looked so easy when she gave them a pill that you didn't think you'd have any trouble, but you're beginning to get a little apprehensive. You know you'll be able to put a pill down your female's throat but your male is such a jitterbug. There's no way you can get him to hold still and at the same time get his mouth open. What do you do now? You could call your vet and ask her how to do it but you don't want her to think you're incompetent. Here is the most effective way to give your cat a pill:

1. Crouch down and back your cat between your legs.

2. If you're right-handed, reach your left hand over the top of his head.

3. Grasp him under the cheekbones with your thumb on

the right and your third finger on the left. Don't stick your fingers in the corners of his mouth. He might unmeaningly take a juicy chomp.

4. Slowly and gently rotate his head upward by using your thumb and third finger. You'll know his head is far enough when the lower jaw starts to drop open.

5. Now grasp the pill between the thumb and index finger of your right hand and place your middle finger between the two big teeth of his lower jaw. Open his mouth wide and the pill should drop to the back of his mouth.

6. Close his mouth and kiss his nose. This display of affection should fly the pill down!

If you find this technique doesn't work for you, try crushing the pill with a mortar and pestle. Conceal it in a small portion of food so that your cats will gulp it right down. Now if, again, you are unsuccessful because they either refuse to eat the food or spit it up because the pill's too bitter, stop there! It's time to call your vet and ask if you can bring them back to be pilled. There's a limit to how much time, energy, and stress you can expend. Don't worry, yours won't be the first phone call of this nature. Your vet won't be overwhelmed!

You just couldn't get the pill down your male's throat. Your female took it like a dream. However, you were able to conceal your male's pill in a bit of tuna. But then you remembered your vet told you that tuna was bad for your cats' skin and nervous condition. You realize now that this is probably one of the reasons why your male *is* such a jitterbug. Maybe tuna isn't good for them but you know they won't eat anything else.

There is a way you can wean them off the tuna. Each

day, gradually start adding a very small portion of a cat food that's primarily beef or chicken or cooked food. Mix it in very well with the tuna. When the mixture is half and half, continue that ratio for a few weeks. Then slowly start adding less tuna and more of the other food. If you make the changeover gradually, it won't be such a radical difference. If your cats go off their food for a couple of days, don't weaken. Losing a few ounces is better than developing a major illness.

A couple of months have passed and they're now eating only a very small portion of tuna. It's been a royal struggle but now it's nearly over. You feel that even if you can't *entirely* wean them of tuna, they've come a long way. You're proud of their nutritional progress but something else has you annoyed. They have two Felix scratching posts which they've always used religiously, but now they've started scratching on your bathroom rug. It occurs to you that they may be doing it as revenge because you've taken away most of their tuna.

It's more likely that your cats need replacements for their scratching posts. After a while, the material wears out and the post is not as inviting as it once was. Hurry up and send away for replacements. When they arrive, just remove the old posts from their platforms and replace them with the new ones. Don't forget to turn each post upside-down and hammer a wedge into the underside of each platform to secure the post so it's steady.

At last you can feel good about knowing *there is a way* to deal with those problems of your cats that appear impossible!

Chapter 10

Why
Do My Cats
Do That?

Yesterday evening your great uncle, who's not too fond of cats, came to dinner. Before he arrived, you gave your cats *their* dinner and some special treats. When you eat alone, they often join you on the table. This, however, was not the evening for a communal dinner. Your uncle would simply be mortified and you'd be embarrassed. In addition, your cats would only get confused.

Well, dinner went smoothly. Your cats wandered near the table a few times but only sniffed at your uncle's shoes. Then they settled down to wash each other. Your uncle even commented on how nice they are, for cats. You ignored his last couple of words and proceeded to tell him how much they mean to you.

After dinner your uncle was comfortably seated in your rocker, which is actually your male cat's rocker, sipping some port. You had disappeared into the kitchen when all of a sudden your uncle cried out. You returned to find your uncle in a state of frenzy. He incoherently explained that your male cat had jumped up on his lap and started

digging his front claws, one after the other, in slow motion into his pants. Besides getting fur all over him, it hurt. As he tried to push your cat down, he dropped his glass and it spilled all over his white jacket. He continued to stammer and sputter and it took a good half hour before he calmed down. You insisted he take one of his heart pills before there was a real calamity. Fortunately, he was staying at a hotel nearby, and he would be in town for a few more days so he would be able to get his jacket cleaned before leaving. You tried to remove the stain with salt and club soda with little success. Your uncle left soon after, mumbling a tight thank you and saying he'd call you before he left town. You would have gotten mad at your male cat if you were fond of your uncle. You wonder why he had to torment your uncle and it occurred to you that maybe it bothered him that your uncle was sitting in his rocker, but you've often heard that cats will seek out anticat people.

Perhaps your male cat was trying to regain his rocker, but that wasn't the only reason he jumped into your uncle's lap. When a person is uncomfortable or anxious about the present situation, his energy level is high. You can sometimes determine this by the way he sits or stands, or by his facial expressions. Often his voice will convey his anxiety. Now your uncle was anxious because of your cats. Your male cat was able to sense this release of energy, and being very high-strung, he had to do something to soften or allay it so he wouldn't feel frustrated. Instead of withdrawing from the source, his choice was to confront it. His method consisted of kneading your uncle's legs, because a cat associates kneading with happiness and protection. This feeling stems from kittenhood. Kittens knead when they're nursing and often this characteristic is carried over to adulthood. By kneading, your cat would feel happy and this feeling could wipe out the anxiety that was coming from your uncle. If your uncle had been able to relax, his port might have been saved.

Not all cats will react this way to anticat people in their home. Some will withdraw or ignore such people. It depends on their sensitivity and vulnerability. You might compare your male cat's behavior with that of a person who was trying to verbally console or calm down someone who was upset and was, in turn, upsetting him. Actually, the best way to console an upset person is by contact (such as kneading). The warmth of being touched does so much to ease tension and make one feel good.

Well, now you know how your male cat reacts to anticat people. Hopefully, that particular breed of person will be a rare visitor to your place in the future.

There's something else you've always wondered about. Your female cat has the most bizarre eating habit. It started when she was a kitten. There are moments when she won't eat unless you pet her. Then she'll start chomping away on her food. But if you stop petting her, she'll stop eating and turn around and glare at you until you start petting her again. When she's decided you've petted her enough, she'll continue eating and ignore you. That's your signal that it's all right to stop. Often she'll purr through most of this ritual and it's hard to refuse her because she's so insistent. It's just never made any sense to you why she does this.

When kittens are nursing, there is an exchange of body contact between them and their mother. The feeling from the body contact is warm and comforting. The warmth and comfort makes both mother and kittens happy. A happy kitten can enjoy his food more and digest it better. A happy mother cat can produce healthier milk and thus healthier kittens. Some cats need the reinforcement of touch to stimulate their appetite and provide them with the warmth and comfort they had when they were nursing. This may be because they could never get enough of this contact from their mother, or it may just be something that they still want and need in order to feel good. There are many people with ulcers who could use this type of therapy while they are eating. Fortunately, your cat, because she's controlled by her senses and instincts, lets you know immediately when she feels the need for you to comfort her. You'll never have to worry about *her* developing gastric ulcers.

Petting brings to your mind another extraordinary thing you've noticed about both your cats. Sometimes one will be all nestled up in the basket fast asleep. In the meantime you might be in the bedroom reading or perhaps balancing your checkbook. Soon the other cat will jump up in your lap and rub or throw himself against you. Naturally, you become distracted, and the two of you become immersed in cuddling. Many times you're not even talking. Well, in any case, suddenly your other cat, who a moment ago was fast asleep, appears so that he can join in on the cuddling. You can't figure out how, if your cat's fast asleep, he can manage to be so aware of what's happening in the next room. It would be different if you were talking or rattling their food dishes.

Cats don't need to depend on sounds to know what's happening. They are affected by what they feel instinctively and moment by moment. The positive energy that you and the one cat are releasing is what draws the other cat to the source. Your cat feels the release of energy, and if it is strong enough he will respond to it. Why not compare it to the person who instinctively knows when dinner is being served. A person's sense of feeling is not so highly and finely developed as a cat's because people depend so much on their intellect. Cats are not intellectually or mentally endowed, but they don't have to be. Often feelings are more accurate than thoughts.

Speaking of extraordinary things, the other day's episode was a fine example. Your female had spent the afternoon in the garden while your male sunned himself in the living-room window. Evidently, he wasn't in the mood for exercising. When your female returned from her jaunt, she went over and started washing him. After a few licks, he started sniffing and nipping her, but this is one of their rituals. You hardly paid any attention until he hissed at her and backed her into a corner. Although you yelled to him to stop, he persisted. Then you stamped your feet, yelled, and clapped your hands—still no response. It wasn't until you took some sliced chicken from the refrigerator and offered it to him that he was distracted from cornering your female. After eating, he continued to hiss whenever she walked near him. You gave them each some catnip and a few hours later he calmed down. He still sniffed at her but that was all. By the end of the evening they slept together in their basket, so you knew he'd forgiven her for whatever it was she did that incited him. However, you just couldn't figure out what caused him to behave in such an aggressive manner. He practically treated her as he would a strange cat.

There was a good chance that he thought she was a strange cat. That's why he reacted so aggressively toward her. While your female was cruising the garden, either she mixed with another cat or somehow sat or rubbed in something another cat had touched. When your female merrily and innocently returned to your male, he was threatened by her unfamiliar smell and was trying to defend himself against it. Although she looked like the same cat, she didn't smell like the same cat, and that's what mattered. It wasn't until the strange smell disappeared that he could relax and accept her in his usual friendly way. This situation could easily be repeated but perhaps with your cats' roles reversed. There's no way to prevent it if your cats are able to come in contact with other cats.

Balzac and Kelly are two apartment cats. Their people frequently let them roam in the hall and leave the door ajar so they can get back inside the apartment at will. One evening a neighbor's cat entered the apartment but only long enough to confront the two cats and then dash out. Balzac and Kelly's people immediately shut the door to avoid any further confrontation. Both cats ran to the door and sniffed it all over. Soon they were hissing and fighting with each other. Their people were finally able to separate them by dousing them with the plant sprayer.

This is another incident of hostility that was triggered by an alien cat. Balzac and Kelly were threatened by the cat's smell and transferred their aggression to each other. If they hadn't been separated by the water, they would have continued to harass each other until their frustration was worked out. After I explained to their people why there was this outbreak of hostility, they decided they would arrange it so that Kelly and Balzac and the neighbor's cat couldn't intermingle while roaming the hall. They wanted to be sure to avoid another occurrence.

Although your cats are different in so many respects, one of the habits they share in common never ceases to amaze and sometimes annoy you. You always try to keep their litter box clean both for their sake and yours. Unlike some friends of yours who are oblivious to the condition and odor of their cats' litter box, your nose is like that of a bloodhound. Sometimes you wish it weren't so sensitive. Anyway, no sooner do you scoop out their box and add new litter, than one of your cats jumps in. Once more you scoop out the debris and the other occupies the box. When you're not home, they "go about their business" as usual. But if you're around, they do their best to try to use it when it's spotless.

Actually, you can use your cats' fastidiousness to good advantage before you take them on a trip. Before leaving home, change the litter box. Chances are your cats won't be able to resist the lure of clean litter, and all of you will be able to travel more comfortably.

Outdoor cats, though they may use a general vicinity for

excretions, will rarely use the same spot twice. It is because cats are instinctively fastidious that their toilet habits are so demanding. Sometimes such fussiness can be annoying, especially when you're in a hurry, but imagine how you'd feel if your cats preferred your rug or kitchen floor to their litter box.

One of these days you'll get around to buying a movie camera. It shouldn't take too many months for you to figure out how to use it. Only if you put their routines on film could anyone truly appreciate the stories you tell about your cats. Last night's performance was spectacular.

You had just returned from visiting a friend who has two female cats. One of them is being treated for a urinary infection and accidently dribbled over your shoes. Of course you washed it off, but evidently the shoes still carried the telltale smell, because after you removed them, your cats literally fell all over them. They couldn't get enough. The expression on your male's face was priceless. He practically panted and his mouth remained wide open, almost frozen, as he proceeded to sniff and lick your shoes. You finally decided to remove your shoes to the closet before they were saturated. Canvas doesn't hold up too well under the best conditions. The cats were at first confused and disappointed after you removed your shoes. But then they started washing, and this led to chasing each other. Suddenly, your female did one of her exquisite leaps just as your male was about to grab her. Soon they were rubbing and bumping against your legs so you would give them their required overabundant amount of affection. You tell yourself if only you could harmoniously work out your moods and energy spurts as well as your two cats, you wouldn't need exercise classes and you'd be finished with therapy in no time.

Chapter 11

Allergies

Well now you've gone and done it. You're having a relationship with a sharp number from Wall Street. Not only is he very handsome, his assets include a town house in the city, a small country estate with horses, membership in the best clubs, and parents who reside across the Atlantic. He even shares your interest in bicycling and yoga. He's practically the perfect beau except for two stumbling blocks. He's insanely jealous and he doesn't like your cats. In fact, he won't even enter your apartment anymore because of them.

His attitude rather puzzles you because the first time he came to your apartment, which was the only time, it was your first evening together. Your cats greeted him at the door and he didn't seem adversely affected. You recall that he made a big show of petting them and telling you how handsome they were. That evening your cats did their usual repertoire, which included getting in the middle of the two of you whenever things got intense, but otherwise they did nothing unbecoming.

It wasn't until after you'd been seeing this new beau for a while that he started criticizing your cats. First he told you that you spent too much time fussing and worrying about them. Of course, you hardly paid any attention to his criticisms. You were sure that once he got to know them better, he'd feel the same way you do about them. But unfortunately, he grew more intolerant and more outspoken.

Now, in spite of all his endearing and attractive qualities, you're beginning to wonder how much he really does care for you. You've mentioned the conflict to many of your friends and they seem to feel you should overlook it. Your shrink reacted indifferently when you talked over the problem, and you got the impression that he shared the same sentiments as your beau. Maybe you should continue to ignore his criticisms but you keep getting a confused, frustrated feeling in your gut. Sometimes it's pretty painful. When this happens, you usually soothe the feeling with food. But this doesn't seem like a healthy reaction and, besides, your waistline really can't stand the extra calories. After a strict diet, you've finally managed to fit into most of your clothes again. In spite of the consensus you know you'll have to figure this out for yourself. You think perhaps if you confronted the issue with your beau, he would have a change of heart. Why shouldn't he, if he truly cares for you and what's dear to you? You'd explain to him that you love your cats and need so much for him to feel the same way. Ah, but there seems to be something that's stopping you. It could be that you feel you might be confronted with the plain truth; that he really doesn't care about your needs and feelings, and you might be rejected. You're wondering if you could deal with the rejection. If only you could accept his annoyance with your cats lightly, but you can't. What's wrong with you, you wonder? Why must you be so sensitive?

If you weren't so sensitive, you wouldn't be half as aware as you are. You probably wouldn't even recognize when people were not being straight with you. There's nothing wrong with your level of sensitivity. Because of it, you can sense that your beau's objections to your cats are indicative of something deeper. Well, you're right!

His attitude toward your cats is purely symptomatic. He doesn't want to share you with anything that takes time or affection away from him. This is characteristic of someone who's insecure. If he has a negative feeling about your cats, you can expect this feeling to accompany any other interests or relationships that you have outside of him. He'll be constantly competing and criticizing anyone or anything you're part of that threatens his security. Your cats have lived with you for several years now and you've shared many growing experiences together. You know they've taught you how to relax better than you ever have before. They've made you laugh at times when you wanted to die. You know that you could never let them down and, if you did, your life would carry the scar. Although you do want to share your life with another person, you know deep down that the person will have to be someone who cares for you enough to, at the least, respect your feelings if not share them. You know you're going to have to level with your beau and, until you do, you're only deceiving yourself.

Very often people will claim that they are allergic to cats, and they can actually talk themselves into developing a rash or having difficulty breathing when they are around cats. Their dislike of cats may have begun because they can't figure cats out or because they can't control them.

A cat is dependent on the people he lives with for his basic needs but, unless he is sick, he cannot be controlled or manipulated. A cat is a free spirit and will not be subservient. People who derive their gratification from giving commands that others must obey can be threatened by a cat. It's hard to assert your sense of power over a cat.

Cats respond to sensuality and warmth. They do not thrive on commands and force. Trying to force a cat to do something is like trying to make the sun shine. If your cat happens to respond to a direction or command, it's because he's interested in doing whatever it is at the time. However, you may find the next time you ask him to oblige, he either yawns or goes off in the opposite direction.

Some people are afraid of cats because of something that happened in their early childhood or perhaps because their parents cultivated this fear. If a parent dislikes cats, this feeling can be easily transferred to the children and manifest itself in the form of fear. If a person truly wants to overcome this fear, it can be done. How? By observing cats in a happy home environment, rehashing childhood prejudices, and very slowly interacting with cats. This process shouldn't be rushed because the acceptance would not be lasting.

Then, alas, there are those people who love cats deeply, who are not psychosomatically, but organically allergic to cats. A true allergy is an overreaction of the body's immune system to the presence of foreign proteins. Many of these people are able to control their allergy by receiving a series of injections to decrease their hypersensitivity. In other instances, aerosol medication can relieve the symptoms. There is usually some relief available for everyone.

It's very important for the allergic cat lover to find a doctor who has an affinity for cats. Many times a doctor will attribute an allergy to cats because of his own prejudices or without really doing the diagnostic work that's necessary. It's not uncommon for parents to give away their child's cat or kitten because of an allergist's diagnosis. The child may carry the traumatic scar for many years after and only later find out that he's not allergic to cats after all.

One client was told by her allergist that her cats were responsible for her breathing difficulties. A second physician she consulted, who was sympathetic to her feelings, was able to pinpoint the cause and treat it successfully. The problem wasn't at all related to her cats.

Some allergic cat lovers have been able to control their skin allergy by pure exposure to cats and the sheer determination of wanting to be able to live with them.

One client made the unwise, desperate choice of giving up her two cats for an allergic boyfriend. Six months later her boyfriend had left her and she realized too late what a grave mistake she'd made. She now has two new cats and her philosophy has greatly altered. There's no place in her life for a beau who disapproves of her cats. She explains to them that they're temporary, whereas her cats are permanent.

Chapter 12

Female Problems

Saturday evening was the showdown. You insisted that your beau pick you up at your place because you had to talk something over with him. Perhaps it was the hysteria in your voice that persuaded him not to object. Anyway, when he arrived at your door he was not smiling. You motioned him to sit down on your sofa. As he sat down, your female cat jumped off the cushion and joined your male cat in the bedroom. Evidently, they felt something was in the wind.

Your discussion was pointed and brief. Your beau said little to convince you that he really cared about you. His eye contact with you was barely existent. His eyes mostly focused on his martini. When you made the painful announcement that you thought it best to end your relationship, his reaction was almost one of apathy. He frowned and asked if that meant he'd have to cancel the reservation for dinner. You told him you'd lost your appetite and, besides, you had the runs. On this descriptive note, he abruptly removed himself from the sofa. Then he started complaining that he was all wet. You thought he was hallucinating until he showed you the seat of his pants. Yes, they were wet and on further inspection so was the sofa cushion. Not only was the cushion wet but you realized it smelled of urine. Evidently, his sense of smell was not too terrific or he would have turned blue instead of just deep red. You quickly washed off the cushion, handed him a rag, and told him to apply it to his seat. Next, you rushed off to the john to take care of business. By the time you returned, he'd left.

You breathed a sigh of relief and flopped yourself down on the sofa whose still-damp cushion quickly refreshed your memory. You knew your ex-beau wasn't responsible for the accident. It must have been your female cat because she had occupied the cushion before him. But why would she urinate on the sofa, you asked yourself? You couldn't come up with any reasonable answer other than that perhaps she was upset because you were upset. However, later that night you noticed she sat in the litter box much longer than usual and hardly anything came out. She usually flooded the litter. When, the next morning, she picked at her breakfast and hissed at your male cat as he tried to wash her, you admitted to yourself that she must be sick.

You tried to call your vet but it was Sunday and you succeeded only in reaching the answering service, which told you they'd give her the message when she called in.

Your vet returned your call later that evening, advised you not to give your female any dry food or fish, and scheduled an appointment for her the next day. Both your cats went to sleep that night with unhappy tummys because they didn't receive their snack of crunchies.

Your female's appointment with the vet went quite smoothly as far as her disposition was concerned. She even seemed to appreciate it when the vet gently felt and massaged her abdomen and bladder.

The vet diagnosed her problem as a case of acute cystitis that was probably triggered by stress. She told you to eliminate fish and dry food from her diet because they would irritate her bladder, and she dispensed three different pills for you to start her on. One pill was to keep the urine acidic, the second was to keep her bladder from having spasms, and the third was an antibiotic to prevent infection. She added that she'd want to recheck her in a week and at that time she would check a urine sample. She explained that you could collect the sample by keeping a shallow dish next to the litter pan and slipping it under her when she obliged. She added that you should transfer the sample to a clean container and refrigerate it no longer than 24 hours before you brought it in to be tested.

You could truly sympathize with how your female felt. Cystitis wasn't a new word in your vocabulary. Your last attack was in London in the middle of an opera. After the third trip to the powder room, you just camped out on the toilet seat. You'll never forget that severe burning sensation in your bladder. Each time, you felt sure you had to urinate and would discover you could put out only a few drops at a time. What really scared you was the blood that trickled out. How lucky you'd brought along your medication for just such an inauspicious occasion. As soon as the opera ended, you had your friend accompany you back to your hotel room where you had it stashed away.

You realized that whenever you were under stress, first you started with the runs and then, if you didn't calm down, the old bladder started up. Your bladder is certainly your stress target. Now your female cat had developed the same problem. You decided it was probably your recent state of mind that precipitated her cystitis attack. It wouldn't surprise you if your bladder started reacting soon.

As far as your female's treatment was concerned, you weren't worried about the pills, and you could definitely eliminate fish from their diet, but to cut out crunchies would be traumatic.

As the evening slowly approached the crunchie hour, you began to panic because you still hadn't thought of a crunchie substitute. In desperation you gave them some brewer's yeast tablets so they'd have something to crunch on, along with a few melon balls. At first they looked a bit confused but very quickly they devoured their treats. You managed to satisfy them tonight but would you be as successful again? Now that your female was sick you especially wanted her to enjoy her food.

There is a safe substitute for dry food that won't irritate the bladder and that satisfies many cats who must not eat dry food. The recipe was printed in *Well Being* magazine, and I have included it here so you can give your cats a go at it. Another one of its advantages is that you can make large quantities and freeze part of it. If your cats enjoy this taste treat, you've solved the crunchie problem.

HOMEMADE MEOW MIX
High protein, high fat, high B Vitamins.

3 *cups rolled oats*
1 *cup wheat germ or bran*
1 *cup lightly toasted nuts or seeds*
¼ *cup desiccated liver powder*
¼ *cup bonemeal powder*
¼ *cup brewer's yeast*
1 *tsp. kelp*
¼ *cup liquid whey or soymilk*
¼ *cup melted shortening or suet*
¼ *cup vegetable oil*
½ *cup freshly ground grain*

1. Mix dry ingredients well. Toss with oil and melted shortening. Add water or milk.

2. Toast on lightly greased baking sheets for 20 minutes at 350 degrees. Turn often to brown on all sides.

Store in airtight containers in refrigerator or freeze half of it.

The days passed without any real catastrophe. You didn't even have a cystitis attack in spite of your departed beau. The best news was your female's recheck. The vet found her bladder in good shape, and her urine sample was perfect. She advised you to continue to be careful with her diet and to bring in a urine sample to be tested once a month for the next few months.

Well, now you could all relax again and start looking for new horizons. You celebrated by sending away for some Felix tuffy mice for the guys and made an appointment with your hair stylist for a permanent.

While having your hair permed, you ran into an old friend who was, of course, a cat person. You told her all about your female's bout with cystitis. What she told you about her female was enough to make your hair curl without the perm you were getting.

She had her female cat spayed three months ago. Even after the surgery, her cat continued to have days when she wouldn't use the litter box, and she would cry and roll around the floor as if she were in heat. At first your friend thought it would pass, but two months later the same symptoms were still there. Your friend took her back to her vet and he said there was nothing he could do and it would probably pass. Finally, she took her cat to another vet. He examined her, took a thorough history of the problem, and diagnosed that her cat had a piece of a retained ovary still inside her after her surgery. He recommended an exploratory, which your friend agreed to, and sure enough found a piece of retained ovarian tissue. This small piece of tissue, which the first vet inadvertently left inside, was the cause of your friend's cat's continued heats. After it was removed, the problem was eliminated. Your friend contacted the first vet and explained what had to be done but he was both indifferent and apathetic. You asked her why she didn't pursue it any further. She told you that she didn't have the time or energy and her main concern was for her cat, who was now in fine shape. You feel you would have tried to receive some satisfaction because the vet was so uncaring, but you reminded yourself that it's always easier to think about what you *might* do until it becomes an actuality.

Because your female cat's cystitis problem was one of your current topics of conversation, it paved the way for other similar stories.

Your cleaner told you about a pregnant cat he had found outside his house and taken to the vet to be examined. The vet recommended that she be spayed and aborted at the same time. He estimated that she was only one-month pregnant and the gestation period is usually 63 days. The cleaner decided that this would be best for Sadie-Mae, as he calls her, and Sadie-Mae's surgery went smoothly. However, two weeks later when the vet went to remove Sadie's sutures, her breasts were unusually swollen. Normally, removal of the ovaries and uterus eliminates the hormonal stimulation for breast development and milk production. However, some cats have a paradoxical reaction and the process continues. It usually lasts a couple of weeks and then the breasts return to normal. Sadie-Mae's swelling disappeared on schedule as the vet predicted.

You left the cleaner's breathing a sigh of relief for his befriending Sadie-Mae and for your peace of mind because your female had recovered from her cystitis bout without any major trauma.

111

Chapter 13

It Could Be
a Medical Problem

Yesterday was a real bummer! Halfway to the office, there was a horrendous cloudburst. *You* weren't prepared. Although the weather forecast predicted rain showers, the sun was shining when you left your apartment. Why did the forecast have to be correct when you were wearing your new white espadrilles and you'd arranged for the window washer to come? Your coffee break wasn't any better. The snack wagon was out of plain yogurt and you didn't get to eat lunch until 3:00. That evening you had a dentist appointment, followed by a visit to a friend of yours who'd just recovered from a nervous breakdown.

By the time you reached home, it was late, your cats were starving, and you suffered from both mental and physical fatigue. As you leaned over to turn on the bath water for a calming, long soak, your eyes rested on a brown, smelly clump. At first you were puzzled but quickly realized that one of your cats had defecated in the tub! You thought it might be because their litter box was dirty, but you'd emptied it as soon as you arrived and the clump was not in the tub then. Evidently, one of them must have been upset about something. If you got the runs when you were upset, so could one of your cats. You decided to give them a bit of yogurt to settle their stomachs. Yogurt always helped you when you had diarrhea. Neither one of them appeared in bad spirits so you really didn't know who left the nifty heap. However, your female seemed less suspect because her rear was clean and it usually showed signs of any soft bowel movement.

When bedtime arrived, both cats climbed in with you as usual. You slept very soundly and were awakened only by the clock radio. As you rolled over to lower the volume, you were greeted by another smelly clump. This one was right beside your pillow and was indeed revolting. Your female was curled up beside your legs so you knew she hadn't left you the gift. It had to be your male because he wasn't in the bedroom screaming for his breakfast.

You started to get mad but instead used your energy for cleaning up the mess and changing the sheets. Yesterday wasn't bad enough! What a way to start another day! You told yourself something had to be bothering your male cat for him to display such weird behavior. You wondered if you should make an appointment for a consultation with a behavioral therapist.

Although this problem does appear to be behavioral, the chances are greater that it's a medical one. Yes, your cat's behavior is strange but, in all probability, it's triggered by a medical problem. If you take a sample of your cat's stool to the vet to be analyzed, it will probably be positive for parasites of one type or another. If nothing shows up in the stool specimen, you might be asked to bring in another. If the stool is not of the right consistency, nothing will show up under the microscope. Most parasite conditions can be treated with pills. Often, the medication may have to be repeated a number of times because it's effective only on the mature parasite. Your cat may have picked up a parasite while at the seashore if he had his daily grass-nibble near the spot where an infected cat defecated. Often a cat can be a host to parasites for a long time without showing any symptoms. Stress usually triggers the symptomatic behavior such as your male displayed. Your vet will probably treat your female for parasites, too, since they share the litter box. If you treat the source of his problem immediately, he won't incorporate this erratic way of depositing stool into his daily behavior.

Tonsilla is a four-year-old, tense, declawed cat. She is the only cat, and her people have a young child. Tonsilla has suffered many medical problems, including cystitis and an infected uterus. Although she was declawed at an early age, she wasn't spayed until she was three years old. Tonsilla's relationship with the child has been traumatic, especially when he succeeded in dunking her in the bathtub and causing her paws to bleed. Being a single cat, having been declawed, and living with a young, impetuous child have contributed to Tonsilla's poor health. In the past year she has repeatedly urinated and defecated on the wall-to-wall carpeting.

I told Tonsilla's people that I wanted to admit Tonsilla to our clinic so I could observe her for a few days. During that time she was started on Valium, which relieved her anxiety. A stool specimen revealed that she had an exotic parasite, and her urine sample contained blood. Dr. Rowan started her on medication for both. Evidently, she had incubated the parasite from kittenhood. The stress from her severe health and emotional problems acted as the precipitating forces for her finally to exhibit the habit of using the carpet as her litter box. This was her way of indicating there was something wrong. If she continued to use the litter box, there'd be no way for her to communicate that she had this problem. Anxiety was the major force for her cystitis attack.

As soon as Tonsilla was started on her medication, she used the litter box, and her interactions with us were favorable. Before she was released to go home, I advised her family to thoroughly shampoo the carpet so she wouldn't be attracted by the smell. If this were to happen, she would continue to use the carpet. Because the carpet ritual had been such a long-term habit, Tonsilla might have a few setbacks. I instructed them to give her reassurance, and with the support of the Valium for her anxiety and the treatment of her medical problems, Tonsilla's prognosis was good.

If Tonsilla's parasite infection had been diagnosed and treated earlier, her "carpet fetish" could have been avoided. Undue stress might have caused her bladder to be her anxiety target but there wouldn't have been the dual problem. Tonsilla's medical problems were manifested in her behavior and it was essential to treat her both medically and emotionally in order for her to get better.

Another problem that often appears to be a behavioral one occurs when a cat urinates everywhere but in his litter box. If the cat is already neutered, his person may immediately assume the problem is behavioral. More often than not, however, it is a medical one. The cat is suffering from a urinary disorder. Emotional stress might have been the precipitating force, but the problem must be treated medically before the erratic behavior will stop. If the source of emotional anxiety can be determined and treated, the chances of recurrent bouts will be cut down or even eliminated.

Ring is a two-year-old altered male who spends most of his day outdoors. When he started urinating on the living-room chairs and on the bed, his people thought he was doing it spitefully. They were sure that it was a behavioral problem. I recommended that they have Ring checked out and examined medically and *then* to schedule a consultation with me. It turned out that Ring had a modified bout of cystitis. He was put on medication and his indiscriminate urinating stopped. When we had our consultation, Ring's people mentioned that a tomcat frequently appeared in their backyard, who tormented Ring. It became apparent that the tomcat's appearance and Ring's urinary problem were related. I explained that Ring became anxious whenever he encountered the tomcat, and his bladder became his stress target. I recommended that they contact the tomcat's people and ask them to have him altered so Ring's source of anxiety would be eliminated.

The tomcat's people were contacted and were agreeable to the suggestion. Three weeks later Ring's people called me to say he'd started urinating around again. I asked them if there was any change in Ring's routine. They mentioned that his urinary medication ended a few days ago. I told them there might be a direct correlation and that they should have Ring rechecked again. X-rays revealed that Ring had stones in his bladder. As long as he was on medication, there were no flare-ups. Once the medication was stopped, his bladder was affected, and Ring behaved symptomatically. Dr. Rowan scheduled Ring for a cystotomy and the stones were removed. By removing Ring's source of anxiety, which was the tomcat, and thoroughly treating Ring's urinary problem, his erratic behavior disappeared. It is not uncommon for cats to have dormant medical problems that will suddenly be triggered by stress. Once both the emotional and medical problems are isolated and treated, the symptoms will disappear because the source of the problems has been treated. Treatment of either the medical or the emotional alone is not treating the total patient. It is the delicate blend that heals.

Chapter 14

How to Introduce a Dog into the Household

It's two days before Thanksgiving and you're all excited. This will be the first Thanksgiving dinner you've had at your own place. Before this, you've always been invited out or you've been away. However, this time you've decided that it should be *your* gala event. You've never been much of a cook but you can follow a recipe.

You're especially excited because your younger sister, whom you haven't seen in two years, is coming and she'll be staying with you for a few months until she decides what she wants to do. She graduated from college a year ago and since then has been traveling around the country.

Your cats are quite pleased with your cooking activities because they've been enjoying all different kinds of taste treats. Oddly enough, your male cat really went wild over some oatmeal cookies you baked. Your female isn't big on desserts. She prefers the different sauces, and it's all you can do to keep her away from the hot pots.

Everything's going along dandy until your phone rings

and it's a collect call from your younger sister. At first you can hardly understand her because it's a bad connection and she's shouting at the top of her lungs. The only word she keeps repeating is "dog." Finally, you can't take it any longer so you ask her to call back so you'll have a better connection. She does and this time you have no trouble making out what she says. And it's what she says that shatters you. She tells you that she's in Vermont staying with some friends who have a ski house and is really enjoying herself on the slopes. That part's terrific! But it's when she tells you about the beautiful big dog that befriended her there and how much she loves him and how much you're going to love him that your tongue gets caught in your words. Before you recover, she's ringing off, announcing that she and Boolah-Boolah will be arriving first thing Thanksgiving morning.

"Boolah-Boolah," you mumble to yourself; must be named after one of her ex-Yalie boyfriends. You're absolutely frantic! Your cats are terrified of dogs. The last time a friend brought her dog to your place, your male cat ran right up the living-room drapes. Your female was less dramatic. She just disappeared into the bedroom closet for the rest of the evening. You rush to the phone to call your sister back and tell her she can't possibly expect to have her dog stay at your apartment, but you soon realize you don't have her number. You love your sister dearly but so do you love your cats and somehow a dog just doesn't fit into your life. With nine guests coming for dinner Thanksgiving, the morning is going to be hectic enough. How will you ever be able to get your cats to cope with Boolah-Boolah? If it were just for that day, you could make them comfortable in the bedroom. But there's no way you can keep them separated from the dog for several months.

If your cats are not used to coping with a dog's presence and energy, the introduction of a dog into their domain could be very traumatic if it is not handled in the right manner. Yes, if the dog were to be a transient in their lives, your cats could be sheltered in a separate room for the visit. But an indefinite visit necessitates the proper introduction. The following procedure will pave the way to a peaceful and possibly even happy relationship.

Before the Dog Arrives

1. Move your cats' feeding place to a high spot (such as a counter top) so that the dog won't be able to reach their food.

2. Provide them with a high hideaway where they can retreat from the dog when they choose.

3. If their litter box is very accessible, purchase or construct a kitty screen.

4. Be sure to trim your cats' nails.

5. Try to purchase a tape or record of a barking dog. You might even tape a friend's dog barking. When your cats are eating or enjoying a treat, play the record or tape. Start off at a low volume. While it's playing, talk to them and reassure them. Don't play it for long periods of time. Let them become accustomed to the sound slowly. The object is for them to become familiar with the sound and not to experience fear with it.

6. Tell them that they're going to have a new friend who will protect them but who they'll have to teach to be calm and catlike.

The Dog's Arrival

1. It's absolutely necessary that a neutral party introduce the dog so your cats don't feel you're responsible for the intrusion.

2. For the first two or three days of the dog's visit, keep the dog in a separate room with all his belongings. Try to keep him in a room that's accessible to the door for the times when he has to be walked. If it's not possible to keep the dog in a separate room, it may be necessary to keep him on a leash the first few days. Separate the room by using a screen or gate that the dog can't jump over. This way they will be able to see and smell each other at a distance.

3. The dog is the one who must be confined because he is the newcomer. It's the cats' domain. If the dog should start barking out of excitement, the new surroundings, or just on general principles, your cats will be familiar with the sound.

4. It is most important that you not lavish attention on the dog. If possible, have someone else feed and walk the dog for the first few days until the cats have some familiarity with him. If you must do the honors, be sure to feed your cats first, and when you walk the dog, let your cats know you're coming back.

5. Try to keep the dog from becoming overly excited so your cats won't be terrified by his energy. After two or three days have passed, put the dog in the area where the cats have been and the cats in the dog's spot. After an hour has passed, switch them back again.

The Encounter

1. Remove the gate or screen, finally, and allow them to mingle if they choose.

2. Don't force them to interact. Allow them to proceed at their own speed.

3. For the first two days return them to their respective

domains when you must leave them alone. It's best to be conservative. Don't take the chance of moving ahead too rapidly and perhaps causing a major setback.

4. Don't sit and worry about every move they make. You don't want to transfer your anxiety to them.

5. Once your cats have accepted the dog, you can give him attention. Until then, it's best for other people to comfort and play with him.

Important

1. It's essential that your cats receive constant reinforcement and support from you. If you give off indefinite feelings about the dog, it will only be a source of conflict for them.

2. If at any time there's an incident, use the plant sprayer or watering can to cool them off. Never jump into the midst of unfriendly animals. You may accidentally become the victim.

Outcome

By the end of two weeks, your cats should have worked out a living relationship with the dog. It may be one of tolerance, or they may decide to accept him as a real friend. Perhaps one or both of your cats may decide to sleep with or on top of him. They may even decide to sample his food. Don't be surprised if the dog takes to washing them. If they're not receptive, they'll retreat to one of their hideaways.

Ideally, it's easier to introduce a puppy and a kitten because they can adapt faster to each other. However, the kitten should be at least three months old, especially if the puppy is large, to avoid playful accidents. One couple adopted a young sheepdog puppy and a seven-week-old kitten. The puppy playfully poked the kitten in the head, causing a fatal concussion.

Another easy combination to introduce is a dog and a kitten. Razzle, a three-month-old kitten, moved in with Nathan, a seven-year-old miniature dachshund. (Her people followed the procedure I've described in Chapter 3 for introducing a kitten to a cat.) Until Razzle arrived, Nathan had always been extremely nervous and overly dependent on one of his persons. He frequently urinated around whenever he was left alone. Shortly after Razzle appeared, he transferred his dependence to her and was able to work out his energy in play. He still turns to his people for love and affection, but the relationship is not the frantic one it had been before. Because of his friend Razzle, Nathan is now a calmer and happier dog. His indiscriminate urinating has stopped and his people find him easier to live with.

Introducing a puppy to a cat is usually smoother than bringing together a mature dog and a cat, but it still takes a while for the cat to become accustomed to the puppy's high energy level. Generally, the cat assumes the dominant role and keeps the puppy in line. This occurs because dogs are pack animals and respond better to a dominant figure. (Size doesn't always determine dominance.)

Sometimes it is necessary to use sedation for some animals when they are being introduced.

Andrew is a two-year-old male cat and Muffin is a three-year-old Pekinese. Their relationship was a happy and peaceful one until their people found Jamie. He was a tomcat and a typical street cat who was wary of dogs. His people had him altered before introducing him to Andrew and Muffin. Jamie's introduction to Andrew went fine, but it was a disaster with Muffin, who tried to play with Jamie as if he were Andrew. Jamie reacted by striking out with his claws. This was especially dangerous to Muffin because of the Peke's protruding eyes. Jamie was threatened by Muffin's overtures and sought to defend himself. Consequently, Muffin became anxious and confused by Jamie's behavior. It was necessary to sedate both Jamie and Muffin to relieve their anxiety. When Jamie's stress tolerance increased to where he could calmly interact with Muffin, their sedation was slowly decreased and then stopped.

Some cats will accept dogs more readily than they will other cats. Apparently, they find a dog less competition than a cat. I feel that it's best to have pairs of animals rather than an odd number. If you have pairs, you avoid the possibility that the two may gang up on the odd one. This won't necessarily occur but there is the chance with an odd number.

If possible, try to find a dog whose temperament complements your cat's. Don't adopt a high-strung dog if your cat is also that way. Try to adopt a dog that is mellow. If your cat is even-tempered, a peppy dog is okay. Arranging for compatible personalities, if it's possible, will pave the way to their quicker acceptance of each other. Similarly, I wouldn't recommend introducing your cat to a hunting dog that's been bred to kill. Don't take the chance of setting up an impossible situation. Bringing a dog and cat together for a lasting relationship takes time, good common sense, and patience.

Chapter 15

Introducing
New People
into the Household

Very soon there's going to be a total change to your living situation. This time it isn't your sister or a passing beau. It's someone you're hoping to spend the rest of your life with. You're planning to get married! You have a good feeling that your cats are going to adapt because they've already accepted him. Besides, he's in love with them almost as much as you are. True, they did even manage to accept Boolah-Boolah. But you're still apprehensive about their feelings and how they'll react when there's a full-time person sharing your bed.

There is a preferred way to go about the introduction. Because cats do not always take lightly to new additions to their household, there is a lot you can do to make the adjustment quicker and easier. Like people, they become used to their same constant environment, and newcomers can present a threat to their existence. You want to be sure

that your cats don't feel that the new person is going to deprive them of your attention, or they will greatly resent him. The feeling you want them to have is that the new person is going to provide them with additional love and affection. If the new person is also interacting with them, they won't have to be competing with him for your attention. It's important to keep reinforcing this frequently, as the following procedure will explain.

How to Introduce an Adult into a Household

1. Before the new person moves in, allow him to feed your cats whenever possible so they associate him with reward and gratification.

2. He can frequently present your cats with treats or toys.

3. Since he will be sharing your bed, keep one of his belongings on your bed. This way your cats will become accustomed to his scent.

4. If your cats like to be brushed, he can brush them and include a sprinkling of catnip.

5. Don't let him forcefully try to win their affection. It's up to your cats to do the screening and the final acceptance by themselves.

6. Plan to spend as much time as possible at home the first night so his arrival isn't associated with your departure.

If positive energy is associated with him, soon your cats will transfer their good feelings to him. However, if your cats feel left out and neglected, they might resort to such negative behavior as urinating on his side of the bed, or even defecating there, or withdrawing entirely from him.

Shooby is a seven-year-old cat who, from kittenhood,

sometimes defecated outside the litter box. When his person's girlfriend stayed over, this problem became more overt. To further complicate matters, because their person is allergic to cat hair, Shooby and the other cat are not allowed into the bedroom at night. Not only was the girlfriend sharing the affection of Shooby's person in front of Shooby, she was monopolizing it during the night because the bedroom was off-limits to Shooby. Aside from not using the litter box, Shooby openly withdrew from the girlfriend, whereas the other cat responded to her.

Treatment consisted of allowing the girlfriend to feed both cats when she visited, making sure that Shooby's person petted him for a while when sitting next to the girlfriend so Shooby felt included, and allowing both cats to sleep in the bedroom when the girlfriend visited. A stool sample was tested, but nothing showed up. However, Shooby was started on medication for coccidiosis, a very elusive protozoan parasite that often escapes detection in a routine stool analysis. It's possible that Shooby carried this protozoan since kittenhood and that it especially thrived when Shooby became anxious and irritated. To allay his anxiety, he was started on small doses of Valium. Soon Shooby was interacting positively with his person's girlfriend, he was gentler with the other cat, and he was using his litter box on a regular basis.

Frequently, cats show their resentment about the intrusion of a new person by such destructive behavior as scratching on furniture, eating plants, or tearing things up. Occasionally, the stress will cause them to become physically ill with either urinary, asthmatic, or skin disorders. Because most cats are sensitive to change, it's best to use the preventive strategy I've described when introducing your new person.

You're probably anticipating what will happen in the future if and when you decide to introduce a baby into your household. Because the energy level of a baby is very high, often cats become anxious and distressed when they are confronted by such a newcomer.

Beau is an eight-year-old male Siamese who shared an apartment with his person and a companion female cat. His relationship with both was very well integrated until the arrival of a newborn baby boy. It precipitated the following problems:

1. Severe urinary attacks.

2. Tearing away at his skin.

3. Withdrawing to the closet and cringing whenever the baby cried.

4. Rejection by the other cat because he was sick and withdrawn.

Before Beau was presented to me, he had been to several veterinarians who treated him symptomatically. Beau's problems became so acute that his person was considering euthanasia. Finally, after much probing on my part, she disclosed that before she had the baby, she'd allowed both cats to sleep with her. Now that the baby shared her room, she locked them out at night because she thought they might carry germs to her baby.

After she became aware that she brought into the house on her shoes more germs than the cats could ever transfer, she agreed to permit the cats back into the bedroom. Their readmission was the major step in Beau's treatment. Auxiliary steps were small doses of sedation and great doses of reassurance. Soon Beau was once again a healthy cat, and once again the other cat accepted him. Beau kept his distance from the baby but his stress limit increased to the point where he could tolerate the baby on a day-to-day basis.

The following procedure is recommended to make the baby's introduction to your cats an untraumatic one.

How to Introduce a Newborn Baby into a Household

1. Tell your cats they're soon going to have a new friend that they'll have to look after. If the baby's going to have its own room, talk to your cats there. Your cats won't understand your words but will pick up a good feeling from you. Most importantly, they'll feel included rather than left out.

2. When you bring the baby home, either you or someone else should feed your cats so they'll associate the baby with a reward. You could even present them with a new toy or catnip.

3. Be sure to give your cats lots of attention.

4. Allow your cats to sniff one of the baby's belongings so they become accustomed to his smell. This could even be done before the baby comes home.

5. Allow your cats to sniff the baby, but don't try this when baby is crying. While the cats are sniffing, relax and breathe deeply. If you become tense, you'll transfer your fear to your cats.

6. Most cats won't want to sleep with the baby but will climb into the crib when the baby's not in it.

7. If your cats choose to sleep with the baby, you don't have to worry about your cats carrying infectious diseases. It's more likely you'll be the carrier than your cats.

8. Don't skimp on giving your cats attention. Triple up!

9. Keep telling your cats that the baby is *their* friend.

10. If your baby is being breast-fed, chances are your cats will enjoy being close by and partaking vicariously in the loving energy.

11. As the baby gets older and starts to crawl after your cats, don't be surprised if they spend more time on high perches. A floor-to-ceiling scratching post is a perfect retreat.

12. It might be best to feed your cats up high so the baby doesn't get into the food.

As your baby grows up and unknowingly molests your cats, demonstrate that this is wrong by molesting him in the way he's molesting the cats. Then the baby will be able to make the association that what he's doing doesn't feel good and shouldn't be done. You'll have to be just as persistent as he is in order to make your point.

Often a baby can create wonderful changes within a cat. Passionatta was always a difficult and tense cat. She mellowed when her people introduced another cat, but she was still distant with strangers. When a newborn baby was introduced into the household, her people were somewhat anxious. Passionatta surprised them by comforting the baby the same way she comforted them when they were upset. Whenever the baby cried, she would sit by and wash her face. From then on, her people knew Passionatta and the baby would live in harmony.

Canterbury and Winchester's people didn't expect there would be any problems when they brought their new baby home from the hospital. However, they did worry about the cats sleeping with the baby. They put a screen across the door to the baby's room at night until the baby was old enough to move and roll over. This way the cats continued to sleep with them in their room and the baby was protected from surprise visitors.

By the time the baby was five months old, she would

move the strings of her booties for Canterbury to play with and throw the ball for him to retrieve. Because Winchester and Canterbury's people treated the interaction of baby and cats calmly and naturally, there weren't any problems.

Arthur and Stanley used to try to curl up in the clothing and blankets for the expected baby. Stanley enjoyed sleeping in the crib and felt sure it was especially for him. When their people brought baby Katie home from the hospital, they were both confused and upset. However, their people immediately indulged them with attention while a friend sat and cuddled Katie. Soon Arthur and Stanley were quite content, but their moods reached a low when the baby remained after the friend left. Their people's impression was that the cats were disappointed that the friend did not take the baby.

For a while Arthur and Stanley were aloof and distant but soon their curiosity got the best of them. They would often watch visitors who came to see Katie and they even appeared to be protective of her. Sometimes while Katie was nursing, they would bite her mother's toes because they knew she couldn't react quickly. It was their way of attracting attention and participating in the activity.

Stanley continued to sleep in Katie's crib when she wasn't in it and Arthur would frequently wiggle his tail in front of her for a reaction. Their acceptance of Katie went well because their people made sure they received extra attention and treats and that they were not rejected because of her.

Sometimes the presence of a newborn baby can precipitate medical problems that are triggered by emotional stress.

Sneakers is a two-year-old spayed female who's always been shy and high strung. Her interaction with her companion has always been more favorable than with her people. She accepted affection from her people only when she was in the mood. Soon after a newborn baby was introduced into the household, Sneakers began to urinate all over the baby's toys and belongings. A urinalysis indicated that Sneakers' urine was normal. However, before the baby's arrival, she did suffer from a minor case of cystitis and was treated medically.

I concluded that Sneakers' bladder was her stress target. The baby's appearance precipitated her anxiety attack, which manifested itself by causing her bladder to ache—even though it couldn't be measured by the urinalysis. Sneakers displayed her discomfort by urinating on the baby's things since the baby was the source of her anxiety.

Treatment consisted of recommending that her people give her positive support and reassurance, putting her on medication to relieve the ache in her bladder, and starting her on Valium to relieve her anxiety. I also suggested that they try to keep objects that might still be a temptation for Sneakers to urinate on out of her reach, especially when they weren't home.

Sneakers' progress report several days later was most favorable. Not only was she religiously using her litter box, she was eating more, and actually coming to her people for more and more attention. She even started to sleep with them. I told them that Sneakers was off to a good start but she might have an occasional setback. Nevertheless, as her stress tolerance increased, her medication could be decreased. It would take a while for her to completely recover, but in time she would.

Often, physicians are under the impression that cats and babies cannot live in harmony. It's not uncommon for them to advise people to give their cats away before the new baby arrives. This is indeed a fallacy and may have to do with the particular doctor's prejudice or lack of knowledge. Don't hesitate to rely on physicians for information about people, but don't assume they can advise you about cats. Chances are you're more of a cat expert than they are—especially when it concerns your own cats. It would be ideal if your doctor had cats or children of his own. Then you could be confident that his feline advice was based on personal experience.

Allie, a one-year-old Siamese, had an ideal life until the arrival of a newborn baby. Until then he was loved and doted on by his people. But when the doctor advised Allie's people that Allie would be a danger to the new baby, they immediately made plans to drop Allie off at the local pound. Fortunately, relatives interceded and found Allie another home. Allie was lucky, but many cats are abandoned through misinformation when a new baby arrives.

Because you and your cats have shared a deep and wonderful relationship together, you don't want it to end when new people are introduced into your household. Instead you want the new people to be included in your existing relationship with your cats so that all of you can live comfortably and happily together.

Chapter 16

Maturity

Nine years have passed and the four of you have had a very tight relationship. Your husband has become your female's shining light and yours is the lap that your male still madly kneads and possesses. In fact, that is what's bothering you.

Whenever you and your husband sit down to converse and enjoy an evening cocktail together, your male always, always, camps out in your lap. But last night was a first! He snoozed in his basket during your whole cocktail and gab session. That was only the beginning. When bedtime arrived, you picked him up and brought him in to bed, as you'd done many times before, but he rejected you. By morning you were sure he'd be sleeping on your pillow. He wasn't! Your heart tripled its beat when he passed up breakfast.

Six months ago you'd taken him for his yearly checkup and the vet found him to be in fine shape. You wonder what could be wrong with him. As you ponder, you realize that he and your female are thirteen years old and now you're really frantic. You schedule an appointment for the vet to check him out that evening. Your husband, you know, is as worried as you, but he tries to calm your jagged nerves and even butters your morning bran muffin for you.

Well, the appointment with the vet didn't make you feel like dancing. She told you that your male's teeth and gums are in bad shape and she scheduled him for surgery the next day so she could extract a few teeth. You wonder if this is the beginning of a whole period of decline for your male or if he just has bad teeth.

True, your cats are teen-agers, but the average life span of a cat is eighteen years old. Your cats aren't even senior citizens. But there are steps you can take to make their days more comfortable and to prevent problems when they do reach senior citizenship.

1. You can start now to build their morale by complimenting them frequently.

2. Try to groom them more often. Brushing is good for their circulation.

3. Start now to give them carbohydrate treats (noodles, cake, cookies). Carbohydrates are the ultimate source of energy when there is kidney degeneration, which is the most common old-age malady.

4. Salt their food so they'll drink more water.

5. Have their urine tested every few months to make sure their kidneys are functioning satisfactorily.

6. If you've been lax about adding brewer's yeast, or Yeast Plus, and wheat germ to their food, now's the time to start again.

7. Make an appointment every six months to have them examined by the vet.

8. Cuddle and hug them even more than usual. They may play hard-to-get, but that's only so you'll try harder.

9. If your cats are obese, trim them up. If skinny, build them up. If one is obese and the other thin, feed the thin one separately. If he's a nibbler, feed him more often. So that the chubby one doesn't feel slighted, give him a tiny treat at the same time the other one's eating.

Many cats do develop chronic problems by the time they're senior citizens and sometimes earlier.

Misty is a nineteen-year-old cat who, at an earlier age, suffered an injury to the pelvis. It left her pelvis narrow and difficult for stool to pass through without strong laxatives. As Misty became a teen-ager, the laxatives were not enough. She has to be anesthetized and cleaned out once a week. Because of Misty's long-term problem, she's always been an unwilling patient and it was necessary to anesthetize her inside her carrier to minimize stress.

In the past several months Misty developed a liver problem. She could no longer be anesthetized when cleaned out because of anesthesia's detrimental effects on the liver. Cleaning her out manually was the only choice, but would Misty permit it? Her will to live is stronger than her dislike of treatment and discomfort. Once a week Misty is wrapped in a heavy towel and and distracted while her rectum is cleaned out. Her person is very supportive and concentrates her attention on Misty instead of becoming upset. With her person nearby, Misty knows she'll be leaving soon and won't have to stay.

Occasionally she has accidents and urinates around the house. Her person now anticipates these incidents and places towels in the various trouble spots. Because Misty's person loves her and is tolerant of her problems, Misty can continue to cope and be comfortable in her senior years.

Big Darling is a fourteen-year-old male with a chronic kidney problem. He's another tough customer to treat. However, with his person's care and devotion, it's been possible to maintain him. When his appetite falls off, he's rejuvenated with fluids, and he's on a special diet that contains a high percentage of carbohydrates. Big Darling has had several close calls but his will to go on and his person's day-to-day positive energy make it possible for Big Darling to forge on.

Icarus is another teen-age cat with a chronic kidney problem. He has only one functioning kidney and a heart problem. His spirit is strong and his people provide him with the love and support he's needed to make it through his major crises.

When a cat reaches maturity, sooner or later one or more of his five senses may be affected (sight, hearing, taste, smell, touch). You must be able to supply the sixth sense which is *to know* how to make him comfortable so he can cope each day with a minimum of stress. The following information can be your guide:

1. Sight. If your cat's vision is failing, do not rearrange your furniture. He's able to make his way around easily because he's familiar with the layout. If you rearrange things, he'll be confused and disoriented.

2. Hearing. It's possible that your cat's hearing may become impaired. If so, raise your voice and make your movements louder so he'll know when you're approaching, or you may startle him. If he's on the bed, gently tap it so he'll feel the vibration and be aware of your presence.

3. Taste. His taste for food may become less potent. If this happens, be sure to feed him more of his special

treats. You might even cook up special broths with bits of poultry and meat to tempt his taste buds.

4. Smell. If your cat's smell falls off, he'll lose his appetite. You can spice up his food with a bit of strong-smelling fish to stimulate his sense of smell. Cats depend on their sense of smell more than on their sense of taste in maintaining an appetite.

5. Touch. You may find that your cat's not as graceful as he used to be. Suddenly, he's knocking things over. When you touch him, he's sometimes grouchy and you can't pick him up and throw him around in your arms without his hissing. He may be reacting to stiffness in his limbs and body or a general lack of energy. You can make him feel more comfortable by massaging him and making sure he has warm, comfortable places to sleep in. You can try to help him reach things when he has difficulty climbing if he'll accept your help and not become embarrassed.

If it happens that the health of one of your cats starts to decline and the other sometimes becomes frustrated because their interaction is decreased, try to spend more time playing games with him (dangling string, chasing, rattling paper bags for him to curl up inside of). A cat is not always considerate of a sick companion. Because his natural instinct is to protect himself against sickness and danger, don't be surprised if your healthy cat withdraws from the sick one. It's not unusual for the healthy cat to sometimes bat or poke his sick companion out of frustration. He just can't understand why his companion's behavior is suddenly so different.

There is no way to avoid maturity in the natural life process. Your cats' maturity will be comfortable and graceful if you can anticipate their needs and do your best to satisfy them.

Chapter 17

Your Cat's Self-Esteem

What a bizarre cat story you heard at the supermarket. If only you could have heard the end of it. Why did it have to be your turn in line just when the woman reached the climax of her story? You tried to keep on listening, but it so happened the checker was efficient and you had only a few things in your basket.

You repeated what you'd heard to your husband and he thought you were loony-tunes. One woman was telling another about her cat, who attacked people and had even tried to bite her. He bit one person's hand so severely that she had difficulty using it for a week. Just when the woman reached the part of describing how she took her cat to a behavioral therapist, it was time for you to leave. You thought you overheard something about low self-esteem but it didn't make any sense to you. Somehow you never thought about whether your cats' self-esteem was high or low. But maybe that was because they never gave you any reason to think about it. They certainly seem to be happy and content with themselves and each other. Of course, a person had to have a good feeling about himself in order to function favorably, but a cat's self-esteem was something else.

Like a person, whose self-esteem develops from infancy right on through childhood and adolescence, a cat develops self-esteem from kittenhood onward.

A kitten needs a fulfilling relationship with his mother. He should remain with her until he is at least eight weeks old and should have healthy interactions with the rest of his litter. Upon separation from his mother and litter, he needs a loving person and his own companion. His person must be responsible for him emotionally and physically. Chances are great that under these circumstances, upon reaching maturity a kitten's self-esteem will be adequate to cope effectively with stress. If there is a deficiency in one or more of these areas of development, there's a strong possibility that later the kitten will be very vulnerable to stress and unable to cope on a day-to-day basis.

If a kitten's relationship with his mother is short or inadequate and he doesn't receive the amount of love and nurturing he needs, the kitten will become shy and insecure. This happens often with large litters where the mother cat cannot devote enough time to each kitten and has difficulty nursing them all. Sometimes, even though it's a small litter, her milk may not be enough to nurse the kittens sufficiently. If a kitten has an unfulfilling relationship with his mother, often his relationship with his peers will be adversely affected. His interactions are such that he's often hyper-aggressive to compensate for his timidity and insecurity. Otherwise he may withdraw and shy away from his peers.

Qatre is a one-year-old cat that came from a litter of several kittens. His people noticed before they adopted him that he was a loner and didn't interact with the other kittens. Soon after they adopted him, he took to carrying around a stuffed toy in his mouth which he sucked and kneaded. He was especially fond of his female person but when he became too happy, he couldn't control his high energy level and he would bite her. Also, he was so dependent on her that he would follow her around and cry if he couldn't reach her.

Shortly after, they adopted a kitten for him from a neighborhood shelter. Qatre accepted the male kitten, whom they named Hodge, on his own terms. Now instead of biting his female person, he took to biting and often terrorizing Hodge. There were times when Qatre interacted well with Hodge and would wash him or sleep with him, but Hodge started becoming anxious and tense because Qatre was so erratic.

Because Qatre had a traumatic kittenhood, his interactions with his people and companion have been affected. His self-esteem is low, and if he is too stimulated, he becomes anxious and threatened. When this occurs, he is defensive and bites or bullies. He's actually overcompensating for his feelings of inadequacy. Although it appears that he's brave and tough on the outside, within he's sad and confused. Qatre's treatment consisted of explaining to his people that it was imperative to give him constant support. By praising him often, they could raise his self-esteem. Because Qatre's people couldn't provide him with all the support he needed, I recommended regular doses of a tranquilizer for the auxiliary support. (Dr. Rowan wrote a prescription for Valium.) As Qatre's stress tolerance increased to the point where he could interact nonviolently with Hodge on a steady basis, the Valium could be slowly decreased. If they were a setback, it would be increased until Qatre could cope again, and decreased shortly after. When he reached the point where his personality was so well-integrated that he could interact with his people and

Hodge without incident, the Valium could be stopped.

Hodge, too, experienced a stressful kittenhood in that he was adopted from a shelter. Qatre's aggressive behavior threatened him and his anxiety triggered many skin disorders. Therefore, Hodge had to be started on small doses of Valium to relieve his anxiety.

Qatre and Hodge's people were able to understand what it was their cats needed and why they were so vulnerable, but it was difficult for them, like so many other clients, to understand why their cats had to be given tranquilizers. They were afraid that their cats would become addicted and would have to be given tranquilizers for the rest of their lives.

I explained to them that when a cat could not cope comfortably on a day-to-day basis he needed help. A tranquilizer provides the auxiliary support that's needed in addition to the care and attention given to the cat by his person. A tranquilizer, when used correctly, is most effective in relieving anxiety. A cat who is receiving sedation must also be receiving support from his person. Sedation alone is not the answer. The combination of the two elements will provide the cat with the strength he needs to break his erratic behavior patterns and replace them with well-integrated ones. When a cat is suffering from continued anxiety, he is hurting. If the hurt is not allayed, the stress often precipitates physical problems. (Hodge's stress target is his skin.) When tranquilizers can be used effectively to relieve anxiety, the prognosis is optimistic. The recovery period varies and there can be no exact prediction about the date of complete recovery. If a cat's problem has been going on for a while, chances are that his treatment will be extended. It takes time to reinforce new behavior patterns, and sometimes the cat will have setbacks. But as his stress tolerance increases, his setbacks will be fewer and his recovery from them will be faster.

Another aspect that caused Qatre and Hodge's people concern was the question of how their cats would react to the Valium. I explained that some or all of the following reactions could occur after a tranquilizer is given.

Immediate
1. Twenty minutes to an hour after a tranquilizer is taken, coordination might be affected. The cat's movements may become ungraceful and uncoordinated.

2. He might feel disoriented and start crying. Because a tranquilizer would make him feel odd, he might try to resist it by running around. If this were to happen, comforting and gentle talk would calm him down.

3. Tranquilizers are generally an appetite stimulant.

Long Term
1. Tranquilizers relieve internal anxiety. As the anxiety subsides, a cat may become more vocal.

2. If he cries, his dosage might have to be increased. Crying generally indicates he's still too anxious.

After a cat's system adapts to the tranquilizer, the above reactions are usually minimized. (Sometimes the cat's appetite and need for affection remain noticeably affected.)

Maggie-May is another cat that came from a large litter and started off as an anxious, insecure kitten. Unlike Qatre, she didn't inflict her anxiety on others. Instead, she internalized her frustration. As she became older, she related better to her people but was still shy and withdrawn. Her interactions with her companion cat were fair but it was apparent that she was tense and unhappy. When she was stressed or anxious, her bladder flared up and she had a cystitis attack. At times when she was frightened she defecated on the rug. Treatment consisted of inflating her self-esteem with praise, small doses of Valium, and recommending a urine and stool analysis. The praise and love were to make her feel good and the Valium was to relieve her anxiety. The stool and urine analyses were to determine if she had any dormant medical problems that flared up when she was stressed.

If a cat's self-esteem is low, he is easily threatened by any change or situation that makes him feel uncomfortable or challenged.

Heidi is a four-year-old spayed, declawed, single cat. She has always been tense and insecure. One morning she became hysterical after seeing her reflection in the mirror. After that she would avoid the mirror and become upset whenever she caught her reflection in another mirror or object. When I questioned her person, she related that she'd given a party the night before Heidi's hysteria and many of her guests had smoked marijuana.

I explained to Heidi's person that marijuana is a known hallucinogen for cats. Evidently, the marijuana affected Heidi adversely. It triggered her hysteria, which was enough to make her become increasingly more tense. More than likely, she caught her reflection in the mirror at a time when she was feeling most vulnerable to anxiety. Thereafter, she associated her reflected image with the source of her anxiety. Treatment consisted of feeding her near the mirror and petting and praising her while she ate. Each day the food was moved closer to the mirror, so a positive association was reinforced. I also recommended that a kitten be adopted for Heidi so she would have her own friend to interact with and increase her confidence.

Bilbo is a neutered, declawed, four-year-old cat. He is outwardly happy and self-possessed. His interactions with his people are favorable, but he often antagonizes his companion cat who's eight years old and very reclusive. His main problem is chronic constipation, which at one time could be controlled with occasional mild laxatives and altering his diet.

In reviewing Bilbo's case, it became evident that his having been part of a large litter did not enhance his self-esteem from the start. The removal of his claws only intensified his lack of inner confidence. His stress target was his rectum and when he became anxious, he held everything in—including his stool. His most recent source of anxiety was precipitated when his family went away for a week. His constipation occurred more than two weeks later, but it sometimes takes a while for the internalized stress to manifest itself physically. During our talk, his people realized that his previous attacks were linked to the times they went away and left him for a while.

Treatment consisted of keeping Bilbo on a regular laxative, altering his diet, and starting him on Valium to relieve his anxiety. In times of added stress, such as when his people went on holiday, his medication would be increased. As his stress tolerance increased, his Valium could be decreased, but he would probably always need a maintenance dosage when he was in an anxiety-provoking situation. Bilbo's recovery was rapid and his people's cooperation in following the treatment plan contributed largely to his success.

If a cat whose self-esteem isn't high has suffered a psychological trauma (stressful heats, tomcat syndrome, abuse) which was not resolved or treated, any situation that again triggers that trauma will cause him to be vulnerable, insecure, unconfident, and threatened. Often, when such a cat's security is threatened, he will attack the source that triggers his anxiety.

Cary is a three-year-old Siamese cat that suffered from an acute anxiety reaction. Because he was a street tomcat, there was no positive way to know what precipitated his problem. It could have been human abuse and the constant stress of being a tomcat.

When Cary became anxious, he would attack people by grabbing hold and sinking his teeth into their flesh. Once his rage was triggered, he would attack anyone in proximity. He could be pulled away only by force. His targets were mainly tense and anxious people. Their anxiety threatened Cary because it caused him to relive his psychological trauma. Then he would have to attack for self-preservation, or the enemy might destroy him. His personality was so unintegrated that he was not strong enough to cope with any stress which made him feel insecure.

Treatment consisted of constant, nonthreatening support, an adopted kitten, and large, slowly reduced doses of Valium. Although Cary's prognosis was not promising, eventually he was cured. Eighteen months later his personality was so well-integrated that he no longer needed Valium. His stress tolerance increased to the point where he could accept all types of people without being threatened. For several months he was able to live in the same household with several other cats and dogs without any type of incident. This would have been stressful for *any* cat. But Cary now had the confidence and self-esteem he needed to live a happy and healthy life.

Boole is another example of a cat with low self-esteem that suffered an unresolved psychological trauma. His first anxiety attack occurred when he reached sexual maturity. At the time, his female companion was unspayed. The stress of being a tomcat, and the added complication of an unspayed female, was too much for Boole. He attacked a visiting person in the house and had to be pulled off. After he was altered, this tendency disappeared. At times Boole was outwardly tense but there were no incidents. He retains a chronic problem of inflamed anal glands, which will often flare up when he's stressed.

Two years later, his unresolved psychological trauma resurfaced. He attacked his person's sister without apparent provocation. His person was both confused and justi-fiably upset when she brought Boole to see me. Judging by his hissing and tenseness as I watched him in his carrier, he was a very insecure cat with low self-esteem. Appar-ently, his relationship with his person was very close and her interactions with her sister made him feel threatened and neglected. When he became anxious he attacked her, because she was the source of his anxiety. It was his way of protecting himself. Treatment consisted of constant sup-port, repeated praise, and Valium. I emphasized to Boole's person that Boole might have an occasional setback. When this happened she would have to increase his sedation for a while and then taper it back to whatever his daily maintenance dose was, once he recovered from the set-back. As his stress tolerance increased, he would be less vulnerable to anxiety. I told her that Boole's recovery would be slow, but if she were patient and supportive, he could be cured.

Lancelot is another case of a cat that became overanx-ious when he reached sexual maturity; but unlike Boole, Lancelot took his anxiety out primarily on other cats.

About the time Lancelot reached sexual maturity, he viciously attacked his companion cat. She was so terrified that she escaped through an open window and plunged to her death. Lancelot's person had him altered. Shortly after-ward she adopted Benji, a male kitten, and a year passed without Lancelot having another anxiety attack. His prob-lem resurfaced with the opening of the terrace door.

The terrace door had been closed for the winter, and when his person opened it Benji ran out to investigate. Something frightened him and he ran inside. Lancelot began to hiss and growl at Benji and would have attacked him if their person hadn't separated them. The next day their person went off to work and left them together. When she returned home that evening, they were sleeping together but she saw signs of a tussle.

Lancelot sat totally relaxed in his person's lap as she answered my questions. She mentioned that when she went away for any length of time, she was told he slept on her bed.

Apparently, Lancelot needs his person's constant support because he strongly identifies with her. His feeling about himself is insecure and he can't cope in any stress situation. That's why he attacked the female cat when he reached sexual maturity. He couldn't handle the sexual energy and took his frustration out on the female. It was his way of protecting himself.

When Benji became anxious and upset, he triggered Lancelot's anxiety. Because Benji was the source of his anxiety, the only way for Lancelot to protect himself was to attack Benji. Whenever Lancelot feels threatened, he will attack. Lancelot's treatment consisted of explaining to his person that his stress tolerance wasn't adequate and any situation that threatened and excited him would cause him to become aggressive. I recommended that she give him constant praise and love to build his self-esteem, and that he would need a tranquilizer for auxiliary support. As his stress tolerance increased, I assured her that he would be able to cope more easily. In addition, he wouldn't be as dependent on her, and his relationship with Benji would become more stable.

Although a cat's self-esteem is first developed in his kittenhood, the circumstances of his life after that contribute to his self-image.

Scythia was adopted from a private party at fifteen months. She'd lived with other cats and had mothered a litter at a very early age. Her kittens were taken away from her when they were four weeks old. In addition, she was not given much attention by her former person. When Scythia was adopted by her new person, she was unkempt and thin. Within two months she was spayed and gradually began to fill out and look good. Her companion was a five-year-old female whom she dominated, but otherwise a good relationship existed between them. Her person commented that she often carried around in her mouth a piece of ear-muff fur which she'd nuzzle. Scythia's private, favorite time was sitting on her person's lap when she was on the toilet. Usually, this ritual lasted for several minutes while Scythia was stroked and praised.

One day her person was preoccupied, hardly paid any attention to Scythia, and lifted her from her lap. Scythia answered with a bite, but shortly afterward appeared stunned and out of contact. Very quickly she became her sweet and alive self. Her person couldn't understand this sudden outbreak of aggressiveness.

I explained to Scythia's person that she felt rejected and hurt when she was lifted from her lap. Evidently, she was used to a certain amount of comforting and objected to being ignored. Because of being low cat on the totem pole in her former home, she didn't have a good feeling about herself. She still had strong maternal instincts, which is why she carried the piece of fur around. Her relationship with her kittens was incomplete because they were taken away from her prematurely.

The recommended treatment was diverting Scythia with a special fuzzy toy or doll instead of abruptly cutting off her petting. If she had something she liked to capture her attention, there'd be less chance that she'd feel rejected. Scythia's self-esteem could be increased by praising her and making her feel special. Catnip treats and melon or pitted olives might help her to release her sensuality. Scythia responded well to treatment but her days were numbered. She became caught in a foldaway bed and her neck was fatally crushed.

Often a cat who suffers from low self-esteem will exhibit physical symptoms when stressed.

A four-year-old altered cat named Shadow lives in a

household where there are many cats. The cats are divided into two sections of the house. Because some of the cats are positive for leukemia virus and Shadow isn't, he lives with the other eleven who also are not. He started to urinate indiscriminately around the house shortly after his people adopted him from the backyard. His interactions with two of the male cats are poor, and they sometimes squabble. At one time Shadow's problem was treated ineffectively with hormones. For a short period of time he reacted by mothering one of the other cats. His breasts swelled up, and he went into a false heat. Shadow's indiscriminate spraying has been a constant source of discontent to his people.

I explained to Shadow's people that Shadow's self-esteem is low and it's hard for him to cope. Whenever he's exposed to stress, his bladder becomes sensitive and he gets the urge to urinate. He overcompensates for his insecurity by spraying as a tomcat would. Recommended treatment was to praise and comfort Shadow often, to have his urine checked, and to start him on a tranquilizer to relieve his anxiety. As Shadow's stress tolerance increased, the tranquilizer could be slowly decreased.

Several days later Shadow's people reported that his spraying had decreased and he felt so good he was even playing with toys.

It would be a while before Shadow would stop spraying entirely because a long-term habit takes time to break.

Rufus is a five-year-old cat whose low self-esteem caused him to pluck away at his fur. He lives in a household where there are two children, two female cats, and a dog. As a kitten, Rufus was very timid, but in the past several months he had become more aggressive, especially about food. Although his interactions with the other animals are good, his favorite person in the family is the teen-age daughter whom he sleeps with each night. Unfortunately, the daughter's interests turned to other activities and she devotes less time to Rufus. This caused Rufus to eat more to compensate for his need for her attention and to pluck away at his fur whenever he felt anxious. As she became less available, he became more demanding and would wake her up early in the morning crying to be noticed or fed. This only alienated her more. She couldn't understand why he was so demanding, and he couldn't understand why she wasn't as attentive as before.

I kept Rufus for observation for a few days to decide on the best treatment plan for him. Very quickly I discovered that he adored being stroked and admired.

The first morning his nurse found a clump of fur on the floor that he'd plucked out during the night. Evidently, he was anxious about being away from home and, true to character, plucked away. Rufus' treatment consisted of constant praise, vigorous brushing to stimulate the circulation to his skin, several small meals a day to satisfy his craving for food, and starting him on a tranquilizer to relieve his anxiety. I strongly recommended that his people adopt a kitten for him so his dependence on the daughter could be transferred to the kitten. As his relationship with the kitten grew, his anxiety attacks would become less frequent and his appetite would level off. Eventually, as his self-esteem became greater, his stress tolerance would increase to the point where a tranquilizer could be slowly eliminated. Unfortunately, they could not accept the responsibility of another cat. His skin healed, but he remains on a maintenance dosage of Valium. His healing will be slower primarily because he doesn't have his own kitten companion.

Sometimes having an odd number of cats can cause hostility among them, especially if one or more of the cats' self-esteem is low.

Timmy is a twelve-year-old cat, Perri is ten, and Amber nine. Timmy was the first cat in the household. He originally lived with another family but left of his own accord.

Cats that go outdoors will frequently move on to another home if they're unhappy with their first one. Perri was found when he was eight weeks old, abandoned in a parking lot. At first he was very timid and frightened, but Timmy adopted him and they became very close friends. Two years later, Amber, an eight-month-old cat, joined the household. She'd been caught up in a tall tree for five days until she was finally rescued. Timmy accepted Amber but Perri was jealous of her right from the start. He managed to tolerate her but there was no great love on either side. Perri had occasionally sprayed around the house. After Amber's arrival, his spraying became more frequent.

The three cats are taken out on walks in the backyard on long leads and supervised. Otherwise, they spend most of their time inside.

Lately, a tomcat has been making appearances in the backyard and cellar windows. One afternoon the tomcat appeared and the three cats became excited. After he left, Perri began to playfully wrestle with Timmy. Amber immediately jumped in and started wrestling with Perri but not in a playful manner. When their people realized she wasn't playing, they closed Amber inside their bedroom. They knew they couldn't allow the two cats together until they had figured out a way to go about it.

Evidently, the appearance of the tomcat triggered the inner conflict that existed between Perri and Amber. Perri's kittenhood got off to a bad start, but he was rejuvenated by Timmy and his people. Amber's arrival was frustrating to Perri because it threatened his relationship with Timmy. Although he was more secure than before, his self-esteem was still low. His spraying around already indicated that his bladder was his stress target. Because Amber was indeed a source of anxiety to him, his spraying increased.

Amber's traumatic incident in the tree was hardly a plus

for her stability. Therefore, of the three cats, Timmy is the pillar of strength. When the tomcat appeared, Perri was immediately threatened and transferred his aggression to Timmy but in a playful manner. Amber, however, became hostile, and transferred her aggression to Perri.

I recommended that their people keep Perri and Amber separated for a while, consult their veterinarian about starting them on a tranquilizer to relieve their anxiety, and, when they appeared relaxed, put them together in the backyard on their separate leads for short periods of time.

A few weeks later their people reported that Perri and Amber accepted each other in the yard, and they were going to see how they interacted inside the house. I recommended that they should feed them when this encounter took place as the food would help them to relax. Within a couple of weeks Perri and Amber were able to interact without incident. As their stress tolerance increased, their amount of sedation decreased. I also recommended that Perri's urine be tested to see if there was a secondary medical problem and that they should try to get the tomcat altered.

Sometimes a cat can have experienced an unsatisfying kittenhood and many other stressful incidents without becoming insecure. A happy adjustment is not ruled out. Also, it is possible that if a cat with low self-esteem leads a fairly unstressful life, his ability to cope will not be compromised. However, many cats are indeed affected by their past experiences, and their self-esteem is in turn adversely affected.

The cats I've mentioned were unable to cope because of their low self-esteem and the various situations to which they were exposed. When they became threatened, their behavior became destructive and unpredictable. It wasn't until their stress tolerance increased substantially, as a result of supportive treatment, that they could cope effectively on an independent basis.

Chapter 18

The End

Sunday morning was divine. It was your husband's turn to serve breakfast in bed. Your cinnamon bagel melted in your mouth and your kitty-cat teapot brought your usual smile. What a fine time your cats had! They hung close to the breakfast tray waiting to lick the butter off your plates and then stretched out together on the woolen afghan. You were in the midst of the Sunday *Times* when the phone rang. It was your old friend Patti calling from Los Angeles. This wasn't a happy phone call. Her twenty-one-year-old cat had just passed on from heart failure. He'd been sick for the past few months and finally reached the end.

You did your best to console Patti, knowing she called because she knew you'd understand. Perhaps that was the trouble. You understood too well.

Somehow you managed to hold yourself together while you spoke to her. But as soon as you hung up the phone, you started sobbing. Your husband, who'd just stepped

out of the shower, ran to you and hugged you tightly while he asked you what hurt.

Very incoherently, you told him about Patti's cat and how it started you thinking of how wretched you'd feel when it was time for your cats to pass on.

When "the end" comes near for your cats, you can only make it easier by accepting death as naturally as life. True, there will be much grief because you'll be losing two of your dearest friends, but there's no way to prevent the inevitable. I've listed the following steps which will help you to prepare for their loss as painlessly and naturally as possible:

1. If your cat is in critical condition, accept the fact that there is a chance he may not make it. If it's a long-term illness, there is the possibility that he may rally for a while and then decline. Sometimes, although a cat may have the spirit to go on, his physical condition cannot be maintained even with medication.

2. A cat's chance of survival is dependent upon whether his sickness can be reversed, whether it can be reversed indefinitely, his will to live, and your support and love. If his condition is critical and one of these elements is lacking, his chance of survival is decreased.

3. If his prognosis is poor but he appears comfortable and not in pain, the end can usually be postponed for a while. By that I mean, if you wonder about whether you should have the vet put him down, the answer is no. As long as he's content and still receptive to contact, there's no reason to end his life. There is the possibility that he may pass on naturally but, if he begins to withdraw or hide, that's the time when he needs the vet's help so he can go easily and gracefully without prolonged pain.

4. Sometimes a cat will stop eating almost completely but his spirits will still remain high. If this is the case, he

can be maintained for a while with fluids to keep him hydrated. You don't want to maintain him artificially if he seems depressed, but as long as he wants to go on, you can give him the support he needs.

5. Often you can tell when a cat is reaching the end when he gets a very faraway look in his eyes. It may very well be that he's no longer in contact and, again, if he's stopped eating and has withdrawn, you should contact the vet.

When a cat is near the end, that's the time for you to be most observant of his behavior. By being totally aware, you can provide the delicate balance that allows him to reach the end when it's his time to go.

Samantha, a ten-year-old cat, had a diagnosed condition of breast cancer which had spread throughout her lungs and was surgically untreatable. For a while she was maintained with medication and her person's constant support. When Samantha became uncomfortable, lost her appetite, no longer slept with her person and companion cat, her person brought her in. Because she knew she couldn't cope with being there when Samantha was let go, she left. Samantha breathed her last breath as her person left the room. Her person was able to provide the delicate balance.

Sometimes cats have problems that can be surgically and medically arrested for a while.

Zelda, an eleven-year-old, had breast cancer that was surgically removed. She was able to live comfortably for several months after the surgery, mainly because of her person's supportive and loving care. Zelda passed on naturally at home.

An eight-year-old cat named Clarence was afflicted with skull cancer. He was maintained on medication for a while. Clarence responded so intensely to being held and cuddled that, although he'd stopped eating, his people were able to let him continue on until he started crying. They were not able to cope with the final moment.

Although Clarence was truly at the end, he still wanted to be held closely. The only way it was possible for me to hold him tightly, and at the same time for Dr. Rowan to be able to reach a vein in his leg, was for me to lie down with him.

I carried Clarence to the back of the hospital to the plant arbor and stretched out with him on the rug. While I held him in my arms, Dr. Rowan was able to inject the anesthetic into his vein. Clarence's last breath was accompanied by purring. There was no doubt. This was his time to go.

When a patient is brought in to be let go, we try to make him as peaceful and comfortable as we can.

While Dr. Rowan injects the anesthesia into a vein, usually in one of the front legs, the patient is distracted by stroking and soft talking so his attention is not centered on the needle. When a patient is ready to go, the anesthesia works quickly and easily.

Sometimes there is no warning or awareness that your cat is ill and he passes on very suddenly. When this happens, it is often very hard to adjust to his loss. All you can do is reassure yourself that you did all you could to make his day-to-day life very happy and, although you miss him, and will always love him, it was his time to go.

After a patient has passed on, there's the decision of what to do with his body. The alternatives are burial in an animal cemetery, or on private property if it's available, or cremation by a private crematory. Usually, the crematory will return the ashes to the client upon request. Burial is simpler in a rural or suburban area.

Many people worry about what will become of their cats if they pass on first. You can provide for this by making up a will and including your cats as beneficiaries. Speak to your lawyer about the best way to guarantee your cats are provided for properly. If you don't want to do this, you can make an agreement with a friend or relative to look after them.

If, after one of your cats passes on, his companion cat is overwhelmed with grief and loneliness, you might consider adopting a new friend for him. If you do, be sure to follow the introduction procedure I've outlined in Chapter 3. However, if your cat is indeed a senior citizen with failing health, another cat might be disastrous. For example, a kitten's high energy level would be too much stress for your cat. If your cat couldn't provide the kitten with attention, the kitten would come to you. This would cause your cat to become alienated and unhappy. Possibly, you could adopt a mature cat with a mellow temperament that your cat would accept. (Again, see Chapter 3 for the proper introduction procedure.)

Joe-Willie White Shoes is a three-year-old cat who desperately needed a friend after his companion Coop passed on from cancer. His person adopted a cat for him very soon after. She followed my recommendation of having the newcomer arrive in Coop's carrier, along with a toy that still had Coop's scent. The introduction went very smoothly and two weeks later Willie had completely accepted his new friend.

Because the newcomer carried Coop's scent, Willie was less threatened and was able to adapt to his new friend very quickly.

From the very beginning, your cats have helped you to experience so many different feelings, both happy and sad. There's no way to determine when the end will be for you or your cats. But you can be sure it won't be easy. If you are able to put as much love and energy into their end as you have into the relationship all along, you'll be able to offer them and yourself all that's needed to be able to cope right to the end,

Frequently Asked Questions About Cat Behavior

Adoption

Q. What's the best age for a kitten to be adopted?

A. At least two-months-old. If a kitten is separated from his mother before then, he may try to nurse you, ignore the litter box, and be poorly able to groom himself or incapable of it.

Q. Is it best to start off with a kitten?

A. Only if you can give him the time and attention a kitten needs. It would be good to adopt two kittens so there's built-in companionship or, even better, to adopt a kitten and an older cat so that the kitten has his own teacher. However, if you prefer mature company, adopt two adolescents of five- or six-months.

Q. What would be the best kind of cat to adopt for an older cat?

A. A kitten, because it is more adaptable, and the older cat will accept a kitten more readily than he will an older cat. Although a kitten usually has more energy than an

older cat, he is less threatening. However, if your cat is even-tempered and has been exposed to other cats, an adolescent of several months or an older cat would do.

Q. Should the cat be male or female?

A. Either sex is fine if you're adopting a kitten for your older cat. But if you're adopting a mature cat or adolescent, adopt a male if your cat is female and a female if you have a male. Generally, there will tend to be less competition this way, and your cat won't be as threatened.

Q. If I adopt an older cat, must the cat be neutered?

A. Absolutely. An unneutered cat would only be a source of anxiety to your cat and might make the relationship impossible.

Q. My cat is very aggressive and possessive. What's the best kind of kitten to adopt?

A. It would be best to adopt a kitten that prefers cats to people. This way the kitten will instinctively relate to your cat first. By the time he turns to you for affection and recognition, your cat won't be threatened.

Q. How can I determine if a kitten prefers cats to people?

A. If possible, observe the kitten with his litter mates and see how well he interacts with them. If he's more interested in people, this is not the kitten for your cat.

Q. What happens if he's a stray kitten and can't be observed with other cats?

A. In this instance, if you're not sure whether he's a kitten that prefers cats to people (a cat-oriented cat), and there's a strong possibility that the kitten might be more drawn to you, you'll have to make sure that your cat establishes a relationship with the kitten before you do.

Q. Doesn't the kitten need my support, and how do I know my cat won't hurt it?

A. No. In the beginning it's important for the kitten to receive all his attention from your cat. It's up to you to lavish all your attention on your cat. After all, the kitten is a newcomer and you don't want your cat to feel neglected or insecure. It's highly unlikely that your cat will ever hurt a kitten unless you provoke the situation by setting the kitten down in front of him and forcing him to notice it. Let the relationship build naturally. Don't try to rush things along or your cat will resist and the acceptance of the kitten will only take longer.

Q. What do I do if I adopt an older cat for a kitten?

A. Even though the older cat is the newcomer, since a kitten is more flexible and adaptable, concentrate on making the older cat feel comfortable and accepted. The kitten will naturally turn to the older cat for recognition. Don't worry about your kitten becoming jealous. If he receives less attention from you, he'll seek out the newcomer more and more.

Q. What's the procedure if I adopt a mature or adolescent cat for my older cat?

A. Don't pay any attention to the newcomer until your cat has accepted him.

Q. How long will it take for my cat to accept the newcomer, and can't I even talk to the newcomer during the adjustment period?

A. It may take as long as two weeks. The less you interfere, the quicker they'll become friends. Yes, you may talk to the newcomer but be sure every time you do, you refer to the newcomer as your cat's kitten or friend. Make sure your cat's included in any recognition you give to the newcomer. However, if it's an older cat you've adopted for your kitten, you should refer to the kitten as the older cat's kitten.

Q. Why do you recommend having a neutral party deliver the newcomer?

A. You don't want your cat to feel that you're responsible for the intrusion. It's best if he associates the arrival of the newcomer with a person he isn't close to. He must feel that you're on his side. The more you champion the newcomer, the less he will.

Q. Must I stay at home a lot when the newcomer first arrives?

A. No, after the initial introduction, it's best to leave the two together without your interference as much as possible. They'll work it out better and quicker that way. Also, the less you worry about them, the less they'll hiss and bicker.

Q. Isn't there a possibility my cat will ignore me if he has another cat?

A. For a while you may be neglected, but just be patient. As soon as the two cats have established a tight relationship, they'll both turn to you for love and attention.

Q. Is it necessary to have the newcomer's stool checked?

A. Yes, so the veterinarian can dispense any necessary medication. You don't want to discover your new cat has worms by having him litter outside his box to get your attention. This is how negative behavior patterns get started. (Refer to Chapter 3 for additional information.)

Diet

Q. How does diet affect my cat's behavior?

A. If your cat is overfed, he may become sluggish and inactive. If he's underfed, he may be hyperactive and anxious. A kitten should be fed three or four times a day until he's six months old. After that he should be fed at least twice a day.

Q. Is it true that tuna can affect my cat's behavior?

A. Yes, because it is deficient in Vitamin E. This deficiency makes body fat uncomfortable, and the discomfort will make your cat oversensitive to touch and highly irritable.

Q. How can I put my fat cat on a diet without starving my other cat? My fat cat gobbles up everything whereas my other cat prefers to nibble and won't eat unless the other one does.

A. If you feed your cats twice a day, divide the food into three or four meals, but put a little extra food into your thin cat's bowl. Once he's started eating, if he doesn't object, move him to a special spot nearby to continue eating. Throw away any leftover food so your fat cat doesn't become fatter.

Q. I allow my cats to sit on the table while I'm eating alone, but I would like to know how I can keep them off when I have company for dinner.

A. First of all, feed them their favorite food just before you sit down to dinner. Feed them something that takes a while to eat. Next, sprinkle their scratching post with catnip and lead them over to it. Diversion is your best answer.

Exercise

Q. Can a cat that used to be allowed outdoors adjust to living in an apartment? What will he do for exercise?

A. Yes, and there are certain things you can provide and do to make sure he gets enough exercise: 1) Provide him with another cat to romp and run with; 2) A floor-to-ceiling scratching post filled with catnip is a good tree substitute. Also, provide a floor model. You can purchase both from Felix Catnip Tree Company at 416 Smith Street, P.O. Box 9594, Seattle, Washington, 98109; 3) Take him for strolls in the hall if it's allowed; 4) Chase him around the apartment; 5) Catnip from Felix, an herb store, or some that is homegrown will help him work off some energy.

If you feel absolutely positive that your cat will not adapt to apartment living, find him a good home where he can continue to go outdoors.

Q. Would it be okay for me to take my cats outdoors for a walk?

A. If you have a strong urge to do this, provide them each with a combined kitty harness and leash. Get them accustomed to the feel of it by taking them for walks inside. After several indoor run-throughs, you can try walking them out to a quiet, secluded spot. If all goes well after a few outings, they may become avid street walkers.

Friends

Q. Why is it important for my cat to have a friend? I spend a lot of time with her and I'm home most of the day.

A. A cat needs companionship with his own species, just as you need people to interact with. There's no way you can wrestle and play with your cat the way another cat could. Don't deprive your cat of a naturally healthy relationship with his own friend.

Q. I have two cats. How do you think they would accept another cat or kitten?

A. The presence of another cat or kitten could set up a triangle situation where two could pair up against the other. It would be easier to introduce a kitten into this situation, but it's best not to have an odd number of cats. If you have the time to devote to caring for them properly, and an adequate amount of space, you'd do better having four rather than three cats.

Q. I have a sheepdog and would like to adopt a cat or kitten for her. Which would be best?

A. It would be easier to introduce a kitten, but the kitten must be at least three months old. Because you have a large dog, you want to be sure to avoid playful accidents by not adopting too small a kitten. You could adopt an adolescent or a year-old cat or one even older if you know the cat has had positive experience with a dog. However, if the cat has reached sexual maturity, be sure to have the cat neutered before the introduction to avoid unnecessary stress. (Refer to Chapters 3, 14, and 17.)

Q. What can I do to keep my cat from getting jealous when a friend stays with me?

A. Give your cat extra-special treats, increased affection, and seek him out if he withdraws. Have your friend feed him, too, so a pleasant association will be reinforced. (Refer to Chapter 15.)

Grooming

Q. How do I groom my long-haired cat?

A. A long-haired cat requires daily combing. You can purchase metal combs of three different thicknesses— coarse, medium, and fine. Occasional bathing is all right, but no more than once a month unless the cat has a particular skin problem.

Q. Is it necessary to brush my short-haired cat?

A. Yes, because brushing stimulates the circulation to the skin and makes the cat feel good. (Refer to Chapters 5 and 9.)

Jealousy

Q. Sometimes I feel my older cat gets jealous when I praise or pet my younger cat. How can I keep this from happening?

A. There's no way to prevent jealousy completely but you can minimize it. When you praise your younger cat, mention your older cat's name so he'll feel included. I still refer to our six-year-old cat as our older cat's kitten. (Refer to Chapter 3.)

Kids and Cats

Q. What's the best way to introduce a newborn baby to my cats?

A. Before the baby is brought home, give the cats something of the baby's to smell. Introduce the baby to your cats when it is in a calm state. Speak of the baby as your cat's new friend.

Q. What causes my three-year-old female cat to urinate over my baby's toys? Is it a behavioral or a medical problem?

A. Quite conceivably it's a combination of both. If your female is unspayed, she's under constant stress, and indiscriminate urinating is symptomatic—especially when she's in heat. Arrange to have her spayed before the habit becomes ingrained in her behavior. If you allow this to happen, you may have to use a tranquilizer to relieve her anxiety so the behavior pattern will be broken. If your cat is already spayed, have her urine tested to see whether it's a medical problem and this is her way of letting you know. If her urinalysis is normal, you may still have to treat her symptomatically for a while (with a combination of urinary medication and a tranquilizer). Evidently, her bladder is her stress target and when she's anxious it acts up.

Q. Is it all right to let my cats sleep with my newborn baby?

A. Yes, if it doesn't make you nervous. If it does, put a light screen over the baby's crib or use a screen door so the cats can look into the baby's room. When you feel more secure, remove the screen.

Q. Should I have my cats declawed so they won't scratch my baby?

A. If you have your cats declawed, they'll be more apt to bite if they feel threatened. You should keep their nails trimmed. Chances are your cats will ignore the baby rather than seek it out if the baby is threatening. (Refer to Chapters 6 and 15.)

Declawing

Q. What do you have against declawing?

A. A cat's claws are more important to him than your furniture may be to you. Even if he doesn't go outdoors, he needs them for balance, playing, and self-esteem. Declawing can often cause both emotional and physical complications. True, a cat can cope without his claws, but so can a person cope without his fingernails.

Q. How can I keep my cats from scratching the furniture?

A. Provide them with a substantial scratching post covered with strong material and lined with catnip. Don't provide them with a flimsy post that topples whenever they attempt to use it. You can either make one or order one from Felix Katnip Tree at 416 Smith Street, P.O. Box 9594, Seattle, Washington, 98109.

Q. My cat has been scratching my sofa for two years. I've just bought him a Felix post but he still scratches the sofa. How can I break him of this habit?

A. Sprinkle fresh catnip on the post. Praise him abundantly whenever he scratches his post. Spray him with the plant sprayer whenever he scratches your sofa. Put the post near the sofa and cover your sofa for a while with material that isn't scratchy or appealing to him. This way he'll be dependent on his post for scratching. If necessary, purchase another post so he'll have variety. Remember, positive conditioning is necessary whenever you see him scratching his post. Otherwise he'll settle for scolding and scratch your sofa because he knows he'll get a reaction from you, even if it's a negative one.

Q. My first cat is declawed and I plan to adopt another. Must I declaw the cat I adopt?

A. No, your declawed cat can use his hind claws to defend himself whenever they romp or wrestle. If he wants to make a greater impression he'll give a playful nip. It is not necessary to declaw the newcomer. (Refer to Chapter 6.)

Outdoor Cats

Q. My cat goes outdoors and, for identification, I've put safety collars with elastic on him but he keeps getting out of them. What kind of protection can I give him in case he gets lost?

A. There's an organization called Ident-A-Pet that will tattoo a number on the inside of your cat's ear. Ident-A-Pet's headquarters is in New Jersey, but they provide a national service. Their fee is about $20 and their phone number is toll free—800-526-4251.

Q. How can I get my cats accustomed to going outdoors? We're moving to the country and they've been apartment cats all their lives.

A. After you're completely settled in your new home and your cats have become used to the interior layout, start taking them for short outings. After several jaunts, you can allow them to go out unsupervised. Try to feed them around the same time each evening so they'll return home for dinner, and keep them inside until the next morning. However, if they're not interested in going outdoors, don't force them. Don't forget to supply them with identification whether or not they are avid outdoors fans.

Q. My cat spends most of his time in our backyard. Lately, a strange new big cat has been coming around and trying to attack him. What can I do about it?

A. Find out if the cat belongs to anyone. If so, explain the problem to them and diplomatically let them know that you're afraid one or both of the cats will be injured. If the cat isn't neutered, nicely recommend that they have their cat neutered so he or she will be less aggressive. If they will in no way cooperate, try to discourage the cat from entering your property. You can try clapping your hands, making loud noises, and even using a plant sprayer. If the cat needs further inducement to leave, keep your cat indoors for a while and maybe the trespasser will lose interest.

If you cannot locate the cat's people but the cat is friendly, have him checked out and neutered if necessary. Finally, try to find a new home for him with someone who doesn't live nearby.

Q. What can I do to discourage my cat from catching birds?

A. You could attach a bell to his collar to warn birds of your cat's approach, but sometimes a cat can spring faster than the bell can ring. Discourage birds from congregating on your property by not putting food out for them. Unfortunately, cats are natural hunters and you can't reprimand them for doing what's instinctive. (Refer to Chapters 1, 7, and 9.)

Sexual Maturity

Q. At what age will my male cat reach sexual maturity and how will his behavior be affected?

A. Sexual maturity can occur as early as five-and-a-half months and as late as eighteen months. His urine will probably smell stronger and he may even start urinating outside his box. His behavior with you and/or his companions may become unusually aggressive, he may sit by the door and try to get out, and he may start howling like a typical tomcat. He also may start mounting his companion and biting his or her neck. If any or all of these symptoms appear and your male cat is "of age," make an appointment for him to be altered. If you have any doubts, have him examined by your veterinarian. Don't procrastinate too long or your male's symptoms may become habits that may take time to correct.

Q. My male cat was altered several months ago but he's still spraying and his urine smells like a tomcat's. What can I do?

A. There's a strong possibility that your cat is still a tomcat. He may have a retained testicle. It could be that the veterinarian removed only one testicle. Perhaps one of the testicles had not descended and the vet removed only the one that had. If this is the case you should make an appointment to have the vet perform an exploratory and have the testicle removed. When a vet routinely removes the descended testicle, then neither takes the time to find the undescended one, nor informs the client of this, this is gross negligence. If he doesn't want to take the time to do the more involved surgery, or feels incapable of doing it, it's still his duty to tell the client that his cat will probably still act like a tomcat if the surgery isn't performed.

Q. Won't my cats become fat and lazy and lose their sensuality if I have them neutered?

A. They will become fat and lazy only if you overfeed them. Since they generally become more relaxed after their surgery, you might have to reduce their food intake. As for losing their sensuality, this happens only if they are neutered before reaching full sexual maturity. Cats don't intellectualize their sexuality. They react on an emotional and sensual level. They are not rational, and they experience sensations by feeling and not by thinking things out. Their finely developed senses control their behavior.

Q. I have a four-year-old altered male cat and a ten-month-old unspayed female. Do you think it's necessary to have her spayed? There's no way for her to become pregnant.

A. An unspayed female is under constant stress and more prone to physical and emotional disorders. Your female's sexual tension can cause your male to become anxious and may possibly trigger secondary medical problems. If you have her spayed, both your cats will be healthier and more comfortable.

Q. Wouldn't it be best to give my cat a vasectomy instead of having him castrated?

A. No, because unlike castration, where the testicles are removed, a vasectomy consists of severing the tube that carries sperm from the testes. Although this prevents conception, it doesn't rid your cat of the hormones that enable him to spray, and he'll still behave like a tomcat.

Q. I have an unspayed three-year-old cat who has suddenly started attacking me, and she also plays too roughly with her altered companion. Is there anything I can do to keep her from behaving this way?

A. Have her spayed. Her sexual maturity triggers her aggressive behavior. Because she can't release her sexual energy by mating with unaltered male cats, whenever she is stimulated or excited, she becomes frustrated and takes it out on you and her companion. Within a month after she is spayed, her aggressive behavior should disappear.

Q. Why do you think my one-year-old unspayed female is urinating outside her box?

A. A sexually mature female often forgets her toilet training and will not use her litter box either to urinate or defecate. Soon after she's spayed, she will return to using her litter box. It's not unlikely, too, that an unspayed female is more predisposed to urinary problems.

Q. When does a female cat reach sexual maturity?

A. Generally between five-and-a-half and fifteen months. She should have an ovario-hysterectomy after her first heat. (Refer to Chapter 4.)

Travel

Q. Does my cat have to be tranquilized for a plane trip?

A. Yes, because of the extreme noise level alone, not to mention the other stress factors. You can use oral or injectable sedation. Check with your veterinarian. If the oral type is your choice, be sure to give your cat a trial dosage beforehand to make sure it will be effective. Injectable sedation is generally more reliable.

Q. If my cat can't travel in the cabin with me, is the cargo or luggage hold safe?

A. It depends upon the particular airline. Inquire about what provisions the airline offers and if possible send away for the booklet, "Safe Animal Transportation in Passenger Aircraft." The publisher is the McDonnell Douglas Corporation, Douglas Aircraft Company, 3855 Lakewood Blvd., Long Beach, CA 90801.

Q. Can my cats have any food before flying?

A. It's best not to feed them for at least four hours before departure.

Q. What's the best kind of carrier for my cats to travel in?

A. Try to purchase a commercial carrier that has a wire top, which will provide better ventilation than the others. If you're traveling by plane, the airline may supply you with a plastic carrier that's very adequate. Whichever carrier you decide on, be sure to line it with strips of newspaper for comfort, and, in case your cats have an accident, they can bury the damage. Be sure to have your identification on the outside of the carrier.

Q. How can I make my cats comfortable if I take them traveling by car?

A. Try to have the car a comfortable temperature (according to season), carry your cats to the car in their carrier, and be sure to leave the windows open only a crack. Take along a litter box to set up in the car and don't forget a water bowl if it's a long trip. If your cats become too frantic outside the carrier, keep them confined. It might be necessary to tranquilize them if the trip will be long or if you feel they'll become overly excited.

Q. Do you have any recommendations for hotel travel with my cat?

A. Put up your "Do Not Disturb" sign whenever you leave your room to avoid someone entering and inadvertently letting your cat out. Inform the maid that your cat is along and ask her not to leave the door to your room open when she cleans. Be sure to leave the room in tip-top shape for the next cat.

Q. Is it possible to travel with my cats by railroad or bus?

A. It varies with each railroad line and busline. Some small railroads allow your cats to accompany you in the car, as long as they're in their carrier. Other railroads allow cats to travel in the baggage car. Some trains don't allow cats at all. Check with the particular railroad you wish to travel on.

Most major interstate buslines in the continental United States don't permit cats. Some intracity lines also refuse cats; sometimes it depends on the whim of the bus driver.

Q. Can you suggest a good pet hotel to board my cats in while I'm away?

A. Never board your cats. When separated from their people and their home, cats are very vulnerable to sickness. The awareness of strange cats, noises, and scents only adds to their emotional stress, and they're a perfect target for stray viruses or bacteria. Try to have a friend stay with your cats, or maybe your cats can stay with a catless friend. Or have a neighbor come in and feed your cats. If this isn't possible, engage a professional cat-sitter. However, don't forget to leave written instructions regarding your cats' diet, vet, chronic medical problems, medication (if any), the phone number where you can be reached or the phone number of a friend. (Refer to Chapters 7 and 8.)

Old Age

Q. How can I provide for my cats after my death?

A. Include them in your will and arrange for a friend to make provisions for them. Perhaps you can do the same for your friend.

Q. How can I dispose of my cat's body if he dies at home?

A. You can make arrangements for a pet cemetery to pick him up and bury him, or you can contact an animal crematory. If you can see it through and have access to private property, you can always take care of the burial yourself. Also, you can call your vet and find out what he or she would recommend. In any event, it's best to keep your cat's body in a cool place until you've made your decision.

Q. My cat's fourteen years old. Can you suggest how I can make her life more comfortable and prolong it as long as I can?

A. Have her checked out by your vet at least every six months to make sure she doesn't have any physical problems that you're innocently neglecting. She might need some diet supplements. Have her urine tested to make sure her kidneys are functioning up to par. Give her special treats, extra praise, and lots of contact. As a cat grows older, sometimes his self-esteem is affected because he can't move around as well as he'd like. Don't ridicule him. It will only add to his discomfort. Although he won't understand your words, he'll feel what you're saying by the tone of your voice and the energy from your body. (Refer to Chapters 16, 17, and 18.)

Miscellaneous

Q. My boyfriend is allergic to my six-year-old cats. What should I do?

A. You could always find another boyfriend. If not, try to find a doctor who's a cat lover. Often there are drugs that will alleviate the problem. Sometimes, if a person is determined, he can overcome his allergy. (Refer to Chapter 11.)

Q. Are male cats more affectionate than females?

A. There is no hard-and-set generalization. It simply depends upon which sex you relate to better and on each individual cat.

Q. What causes my cat to twitch her back from time to time?

A. Cats often twitch their back or tail when they're anxious, upset, or uncomfortable.

Q. Is there anything I can do to keep my cat from urinating and defecating outside his litter box?

A. Have his stool and urine tested by your vet to see if there are any medical problems. Sometimes you may have to repeat the tests a few times to be sure. Clean the box frequently—that is, scoop out the debris several times a day. Your cat may be objecting to poor sanitation. Try using a different kitty litter. If your cat is not neutered, this may be her way of indirectly convincing you it's time. After you've checked all these possibilities, make sure you thoroughly remove the scent from any of her favorite depositing spots with a strong, pleasant-smelling shampoo. Otherwise the smell will draw her back to the scenes of her crime. (Refer to Chapter 13.)

Q. My cat frequently has skin problems. Do you think it's emotional?

A. It's possible that the problem started from emotional stress, which triggered the skin disorder. Various stress factors include declawing, boredom, frustration, lack of attention, reaching sexual maturity and not being neutered, improper diet, and low self-esteem. Have your cat's skin problems treated by a veterinarian and if medicine and change of diet (diagnostic tests, if deemed necessary) don't solve the problem, consult a behavioral therapist. Tranquilization may be necessary to relieve your cat's anxiety. (Refer to Chapters 2, 4, 6, 12, 14, 15, and 17.)

Q. Why does my cat sometimes chase its tail and then start biting at himself?

A. Your cat may be trying to tell you that his anal glands are full and have to be squeezed by his veterinarian, or it may be a minor type of convulsion. Either way, such symptoms are usually triggered by stress. It's essential to treat the problem both medically and emotionally so your cat's behavior will become well integrated.

Q. Sometimes I think my cats do things for spite. What do you think about this?

A. If they're acting purely out of spite, you must be doing something that's making them anxious or uncomfortable. If you think about this for a while, you'll probably realize what it is you're doing that's frustrating them. However, their problem may be medical and their way of communicating it to you can only be done in a negative manner to attract your attention. (Refer to Chapters 10 and 13.)

Pregnancy

Q. I found a stray pregnant cat and had her aborted and spayed. Do you think this was all right? Will it affect her personality?

A. You did the best thing for her. Maybe she would have been a good mother—but who knows! You did not damage her personality, and her sensuality will remain intact.

Q. I allowed my female cat to have one litter because I was told this was the best thing to do. It took her several months to return to her old self. What do you make of this?

A. Motherhood is not a necessity for cats. The world is full of unwanted and abandoned kittens—not to mention pregnant, abandoned females. Many times female cats endure such an exceptional amount of emotional and physical stress during the course of motherhood that it does affect their personality adversely. It's much easier to adopt a companion for your cat than to help create one. The only way you can be sure that all your cat's kittens will be properly provided for is to keep them yourself. However, this is not the most practical answer, and your female cat may not always thrive on this arrangement. (Refer to Chapters 4 and 12.)

Q. Does a cat have feelings?

A. Yes, absolutely. Most of his behavior is based on his feelings and his sensitivity is often more highly developed than a person's. (Refer to Chapters 10 and 17.)

Q. Is there any way to notice that my cat is getting sick by the way he behaves?

A. Yes, if his litter-box habits suddenly become erratic, if he vomits frequently, loses his appetite for a couple of meals, refuses contact, and if he hides out. Another thing you should be aware of is your cat's breathing. If it's apparent that your cat is having difficulty breathing for any length of time, and you can't attribute it to heat or any isolated stress situation that you can control, you should be sure to make an appointment with the vet to have your cat checked out. Your cat's eyes are a good indicator of how he's feeling. Unless he has eye problems, if you notice a far-off look in his eyes, or a look of distress, and it continues, chances are your cat is not well or he's about to come down with something. (Refer to Chapters 10, 13, 16, and 18.)

Q. What can I do to keep my cat from ruining my plants?

A. If your cat is a plant fancier, try hanging your plants out of his reach. You might try squirting him with the plant sprayer when you catch him in the act. However, it may be that you'll have to find new and safer homes for the plants that he just cannot resist. (Refer to Chapter 1.)

Q. How can I keep my cats from tearing up the garbage?

A. Move it to a cabinet so it's out of reach or try hanging it on a rope apparatus. Remember—out of sight is often out of mind. (Refer to Chapter 1.)

Q. What can I do if I find a stray cat?

A. If you already have a cat, make sure to keep the newcomer separate from your cat. Put up signs around the neighborhood telling of your find. If you do not locate the cat's person, then, if you can, have him checked out by the vet. You might want to keep the cat yourself. (If so, follow outlined procedure in Chapter 3.) If you don't want to keep him, try to find a good home for him by advertising in the newspaper, asking friends, and putting up signs in your local supermarkets. If the cat is adopted by someone you don't know well, be sure to deliver him to his new home so you'll know where he's going. (Refer to Chapter 1.)

Q. Do you recommend giving cats catnip?

A. Yes, generally it makes them feel good. At first they may be very active, but soon they'll relax and feel good after working out their energy. Occasionally, it causes a cat to become too excited because the cat can't handle the amount of energy. (Refer to Chapter 4.)

Q. If my cat has to take Valium, won't he become addicted?

A. Not if you follow your veterinarian's directions. If

your cat is taking Valium because of a behavioral problem, be sure to combine it with the emotional support your behaviorist recommends. It's the combination of the two forces that alleviates the problem. (Refer to Chapter 17.)

Q. What causes my cat, sometimes out of nowhere, to suddenly bite me?

A. His biting is probably triggered by his high energy level. A companion cat would be an ideal outlet for him. (Refer to Chapter 2.)

Q. Why is it that my cats are always attracted to people that don't like them?

A. Cats respond to the feelings of anxiety and discomfort that anticat people often experience. Some cats confront the anxiety by trying to make the people feel better, so they in turn will feel relaxed. They may jump up on such a person's lap and start purring or kneading away. (Refer to Chapter 10.)

Q. Why does my four-year-old cat adore kneading away at my chest and sucking on my sweater?

A. Happiness can cause him to do this. It's a response carried over from when he was nursing. Most kittens knead and nurse. Consider yourself lucky that he associates chest kneading with the happiness and gratification he received from nursing. You could always trim his nails to keep from getting punctured. Maybe you can give him his own woolen object to suck on as he kneads. Only make sure he doesn't try to devour it. (Refer to Chapter 10.)

Q. Do you think a cat is affected by his name?

A. Yes—because certain names are associated with different bodily and emotional feelings. For instance, if you named your cat "Ugly," you would say it in a distasteful and unpleasing way because of the word's connotation. Whenever you called him or spoke to him, you would be giving off negative feelings. Because cats are very in tune to feelings, he would pick up your negativity. It's much easier to give your cat a name to which you have a good association and that fits your cat's personality. (Refer to Chapter 10.)